T0196155

PRODUCER AND ORGANIZATIONAL DECISION-MAKING

Is Behavioral Economics Losing Its Way?

HUGH SCHWARTZ

ARCHWAY
PUBLISHING

Archway Publishing books may be ordered through booksellers or by contacting:

Archway Publishing
1663 Liberty Drive
Bloomington, IN 47403
www.archwaypublishing.com
1 (888) 242-5904

ISBN: 978-1-4808-6206-7 (sc)
ISBN: 978-1-4808-6205-0 (e)

Library of Congress Control Number: 2018904618

Print information available on the last page.

Archway Publishing rev. date: 4/27/2018

Contents

Preface and Acknowledgments

This short book was prompted by my realization, given the current interest in Steve Jobs, Elon Musk, and Jeff Bezos, that despite its promise, the field known as behavioral economics is ignoring what those entrepreneurs have accomplished. I had long been aware that after the first year of the major recession that began in late 2008, the leaders in behavioral economics were no longer being interviewed as much about how to extricate the country from the recession and move it forward, but somehow that did not register—even though I had been thinking about behavioral factors for decades and had been writing about them since the 1980s. Then it suddenly hit me, and I was prompted to prepare a short paper, "How Behavioral Economics Lost Its Way," and send it to several who are prominent in the behavioral economics community. One of the leaders in the field e-mailed back that he agreed with the essence of what I had written, but given what I had to say about the findings of behavioral economics and its applications, he did not think that the title was appropriate. Thus the change in the title, somewhat altering the emphasis.

In the meantime, I submitted the original paper to the Society for Advancement of Behavioral Economics (SABE) for the conference in July 2017 in Newcastle, Australia, and it was accepted. At the same time, I wrote to the representative of a major publisher, indicating that perhaps I did have something that they might be interested in. I sent him a copy of the paper. He was favorably impressed, as was a review committee, which recommended publication as a book. I agreed but hesitated when that academically oriented company sent a contract calling for a manuscript more than double the size of the present book. Attendance at the SABE Conference convinced me that the need was to reach not only to behavioral economists but also MBAs and generalists, in order to pressure behavioral economists to change their ways and undertake a different approach to their studies. The representative to whom I had written sensed that I felt this way and was understanding when I informed him that I'd decided to seek to publish a different type of a book elsewhere. I would like to express my gratitude to him and that publisher's review committee, which made several suggestions that I have incorporated into the present book. I also am grateful to Morris Altman, Nathan Berg, and the handful of attendees at the SABE Conference in Australia who reacted favorably to my basic thesis, as well as to the aforementioned leader of the behavioral economics community who felt that I did in fact have a message to communicate.

Beyond that, I am in debt to my wife, Maria Rosa Schwartz, for a number of suggestions. Belated thanks goes to a close relative, the late Preston Beyer, an industrialist who cautioned me years ago to be skeptical of what economists who had rarely been inside a factory had to say about industry. I am also indebted to noneconomists Rodolfo La Maestra and Tom Ferguson for several of their comments. And I am very much indebted to the editors of Archway Publishing, especially David N. Shaw, many of whose comments I have incorporated into the text.

Finally, I am pleased to acknowledge the permission given to me by the Taylor and Francis Group, through the Copyright Clearance Center, to include material from my chapter "In-depth Interviews as a Means of Understanding Economic Reasoning" in Morris Altman's *Handbook of Contemporary Behavioral Economics: Foundations and Developments* (M. E. Sharpe, 2006).

Introduction

Why in the world do economists assume that people usually seek the best that's available—what's optimal, in some sense—and that they (or the winners among them) are successful in obtaining it? That's obviously not always the case, and it's why so much of the public has ignored what economics has had to say over the years.

But along came Richard Thaler, the father of behavioral economics, together with the others who created the field.[1] Behavioral economics is descriptive economics; it shows that consumers do not always try to do what's best for themselves and are not always successful in what they do attempt. Behavioral economics replaces the traditional economic assumption of optimal, maximizing behavior with that of the actual, often less-than-maximizing behavior that everyday events reveal and that studies confirm. It's not just that individuals are kindhearted and consider the impact on others (as sometimes occurs), or that governments and other organizations must resort to some form of nudging to get consumers to do what's best for themselves (or at any rate, to do what those organizations seek).

Is it really true that all consumers tend to ignore what's best for them, or that they lack the wherewithal to attain the best that's possible? Even more important is what happens when many producers and collective investors also fall short, but some outliers do not and so become dominant in their field? Don't we need a theory of economic behavior that deals with such cases, or that at least acknowledges that the phenomenon may occur? It seems to be an important factor of the real world we live in, after all. And speaking of producers and investors, suppose a few individuals make the decisions (which may change over time), whereas most of us simply accept what they determine, more or less going along with what is decided. Then don't we need a special theory of behavior that deals with how those decisions are made and addresses the efforts to get others to go along and implement the decisions?

Isn't behavioral economics losing its way by focusing on consumers alone (and on average consumer behavior at that) and by largely ignoring producers (and collective investors)—or, what is even more disturbing, by assuming that the latter act in the same way and have the same shortcomings as consumers? True, the behavior of the producers and collective investors may have quite a bit to do with the way in which consumers behave and the way in which a society functions. Yet it may help to ask decision makers about what explains their decision-making, and it may be necessary to observe the decision-making process.

The thrust of this presentation is the need for studies in behavioral economics to examine more carefully the behavior of organizations—producers, nonprofits, and government entities— and to explain the essence of decisions that are made as the context changes and as the size and relative importance of enterprises changes.

These are some of the concerns of this book, and the failure to consider them helps answer the question of whether behavioral economics, the description of actual decision-making, is losing its way.

CHAPTER 1

Background

Behavioral economics is descriptive economics, it is claimed; it describes the results of actual human decision-making. This chapter deals with the difference between the traditional approach to economic analysis and behavioral economics.

If behavioral economics describes actual human decision-making, how is it that the field had so little to offer in extricating us from the most serious and prolonged recession of recent times? Moreover, how can we explain the striking success of entrepreneurs like Steve Jobs, Elon Musk, and Jeff Bezos, whose decision-making seems to have been very nearly maximizing, running counter to many of the much-less-than optimal findings of behavioral economics outlined in chapter 2? Never mind that there are other individuals, well described by the empirical findings of behavioral economics, who have fallen by the wayside or have barely achieved even meager results. Is it that traditional economics was right in declaring that the models of the discipline need not concern themselves with accuracy in describing human decision-making, but only with the predictions of the models? Or is it that we need at least two behavioral models? One of these indeed would be limited with respect to traditional economic rationality, and that is the one that would apply for most of us and most of our transactions, certainly as consumers and individual investors. The other (or others) might be more along the lines of traditional economic rationality, reflecting few exceptions to optimal maximizing behavior (though not always the same exceptions). Moreover, the enterprises that correspond to the more maximizing model might not so much be taking advantage of human frailties as simply ignoring them—and becoming more dominant in their industry in the process. (Perhaps we need more than two models of economic behavior if we are to take account of producer behavior, as well as consumer behavior and the behavior of many organizations.)

Behavioral economics is much in the media these days, as is its offspring, behavioral finance. The most recent Nobel Prize in economics was awarded for work in behavioral economics, as have several others in recent years. The field has been among the most prolific fields of economic and business research: special government agencies devoted to the implementation of a behavioral approach have emerged in Great Britain and other countries, and economic policy has been influenced increasingly in both the private and public spheres. Academic instruction is being revised to take account of the contributions of the field, and behavioral economics has recently been the subject of a vast and almost magisterial more-than-1,700-page overview.[2] With all the recent applications of a behavioral approach (even in fields such as medicine), how can one begin to suggest that behavioral economics is losing its way?

Yet there is little question that that is what is happening. Consider what was anticipated for the analysis of economic behavior just a generation back (at least by some): the replacement of the apparently dubious maximization model by one that allowed for the introduction of a broader set of objectives that would apply to all types of entities, and thus would better explain and predict everyday events. The inclination of most behavioral economists to ignore what might be regarded as a relevant type of research (which has been defended by an economist with recognized methodological credentials), combined with the field's inability to deal with either the steep recession recently experienced or the stunning success of several major business entrepreneurs and their organizations in the last few decades, underscore the disappointment over what behavioral economics has been achieving. (Now under way is a move to claim that the behavioral approach is not a serious threat, and that it does not represent a philosophical break after all but is only a pragmatic means of considering alternative policy measures. The claim is that the behavioral approach is no more than another element in the economist's toolbox to take account of in some cases but not others.)[3]

There have always been a handful of economists, along with many more from outside the field, who have expressed their concerns about the basic assumptions of economic theory: that individuals and economies maximize financial incentives, or that they usually perform as if they or the survivors among them are attempting to do so, and that (for the most part) they are able to maximize or come close to it—in the long run, at least. For many years, the best work of the doubting type (by Herbert Simon and his colleagues) focused on the limited capability of individuals to deliver on the objective of maximization, given the difficult task of search (the search for the data necessary for a satisfactory solution), the limits of human decision-making capability, the multiplicity of human and organizational objectives, and their shifts over time in the light of experience along with the numerous institutional barriers.[4] Certainly one of the underlying questions was whether it was financial incentives that individuals, organizations, and economies were trying to optimize, or whether it was a bundle of objectives that included some that, in most circumstances, had little to do with financial considerations (as Robert Frank has emphasized, with his insistence that some deviations from optimization are indeed intended, particularly in the case of individuals). In addition, there was always the academically overlooked tradition of what George Akerlof and Robert Shiller have called *Phishing for Phools*, whereby some individuals and organizations took advantage of matters that clearly were not in the interest of those with whom they came into contact, and that had adverse consequences for the community at large, as well as for those unfortunate individuals with whom the perpetrators came into contact.[5] But surely such apparently deviant, and fortunately less successful approaches, cannot be the basis for revising the assumptions of the general model of economic behavior.

Foremost among the economists who have dissented from the mainstream in recent decades have been those who have characterized themselves as behavioral economists, and it is from this group and the behavioral decision theorists of psychology that experiments and other empirical studies have emerged, which cast doubt on what most practitioners had regarded as the basic maximizing assumptions underlying mainstream economics. The psychologists Daniel Kahneman and Amos Tversky gave impetus to the analysis of modern behavioral decision-making with a heuristics and biases approach that underscored several major considerations. (Gerd Gigerenzer and associates have offered a somewhat different alternative, but more on that later; for now, it is enough to indicate that that approach also involved the reinsertion of psychology into economics.) Kahneman and Tversky undertook and encouraged experiments that provided a seemingly scientific basis that previously had been missing from most of the behavioral discussions of decision-making; the approach was supported by the contributions of Paul Slovic and Sarah Lichtenstein on preference reversal that began a few years before.[6] Initially, some of the laboratory experiments came from experimental economists who principally sought to verify tenets of traditional microeconomic theory but found, as the emerging group of behavioral decision theorists had been maintaining, that the results of their experiments did not always confirm what economic theory assumed to be true (and that the efficient market theorists had strongly proclaimed for several decades). This led to a dramatic increase in the number of economists conducting experiments that contributed to the body of behavioral economics.[7]

If one wanted to use economics first to describe past behavior, then to predict future behavior, and ultimately to use that prediction to influence economic policy, the results of the empirical work of behavioral economics should be taken into account. Publication of work in behavioral economics, which was quite difficult at first (sometimes denied because of its allegedly heretical nature), became easier and increasingly accessible to those who could benefit from its findings. In the process, this made believers of many economists, who had been taught differently and had been inclined to begin their theorizing along lines that many of them did not really believe deep down—as their consulting recommendations tended to confirm— but that they had come to assume as a plausible starting point. Many, but by no means all, economists were inclined to abandon the traditional assumptions.[8] Nonetheless, many of those who had been convinced remained unsure of how to incorporate a behavioral approach to their own work (e.g., exactly what nonmaximizing assumptions to introduce at the various points of their analyses), and the increasingly arcane nature of much of the work in behavioral economics did not seem to alter that.

The empirical findings prevailed, particularly those of the laboratory, but also the so-called natural experiments from the real world, along with a number of financial studies. Even so, despite the increasing intellectual acceptance of a behavioral approach, that acceptance of the results of laboratory and field results and the studies of financial aggregates—*and those results alone, to the exclusion of partially contrary findings emerging from interview-based studies*—is how behavioral economics might be seen to be losing its way. (Not that the available alternatives provided a complete answer, however, as I will explain later.) Alternatives to the established techniques,

notably results based on interviews with decision makers that tried to
discern why the latter actually made their decisions, were dealt with
summarily, to the extent they were dealt with at all. The alternatives
were small in number and sometimes undertaken by those less
skilled in employing experimental techniques and less focused on
financial matters, and they were derided as too time-consuming and
unscientific.[9] The interview-based studies of decision makers that
attempted to determine why the latter made the decisions that they
did offered the promise of fulfilling the early promise of behavioral
economics: that of replacing prevailing maximizing models of
economic behavior with more realistic hypotheses (those reflecting
actual behavior) that would predict better not only for consumers
but for a wide variety of enterprises and for the economy as a whole.

Behind the acceptance of the behavioral findings regarding
human decision-making seems to be the willingness of many to
accept the notion that economics should focus on average behavior.
The implicit conclusion seems to be that the decision-making of
statistical outliers ordinarily does not matter much, that it apparently
amounts to no more than the existence of black swans, and that
it is only rarely of consequence in the real world. Moreover, and
of great importance, there seems to be a belief that what holds for
individuals is also true for organizations, with the decision-making
of those organizations remaining essentially the same, even as those
organizations change in size and complexity, as societal contexts
vary, and indeed even when there is little or no decision-making
input from most of the individuals within the organizations, as is
often the case.

CHAPTER 2

The Evolution of Behavioral Economics

Psychology once played a more important role in economic analysis than in the years since World War II. It seemed to be the case at certain points in time for Adam Smith and for several of the economists from the nineteenth and early twentieth centuries, but psychological considerations are not what those earlier contributors to economics are most remembered for. In any event, the general acceptance of economists of psychological contributions took place at a time when formal work in the latter discipline was in its infancy. That began to change as psychology matured, and by the end of the nineteenth century, the divorce was very nearly complete. The contribution of Leon Walras solidified matters; the acceptance and incorporation of mathematics into economic analysis, and its capacity for producing quantitative and what seemed to be plausible (rational) results, appeared to terminate matters. If there was any further question, it was eliminated by the publications of Paul Samuelson and others dealing with revealed preferences. True, John Maynard Keynes wrote of "animal spirits" and appears to have been guided by them in his personal successes. Although that theme has been resurrected in a recent book,[10] that is certainly not what he is most remembered for. Important dissents were registered, such as those by economists Thorstein Veblin, James Duesenberry, Harvey Leibenstein (and perhaps the list should include Fred Hirsch and Robert Frank), but they simply did not register, at least not at the time they were made.[11]

The proof posted by Maurice Allais at a conference of economists in the early 1950s that individuals made decisions that violated the axioms of economics, then recently expounded by John Von Neumann and Oskar Morgenstern in *The Theory of Games and Economic Behavior* (in this case, violation of what has been referred to as the independence axiom) was ignored by economists, including some who one might have expected to reason better. A few years later, Daniel Ellsberg indicated that the source of uncertainty between choices can affect an outcome, contrary to what rational behavior would indicate, but this too was largely ignored.[12] Tom Schelling's nontraditional applications of game theory were taken into account, but perhaps principally with respect to its applications to the Cold War between Russia and the West. What might have been significant contributions by prominent, mainstream economists such as Jacob Marschak, Roy Radner, and Harry Markowitz were not so regarded, apparently even by the authors themselves. In the case of Markowitz, that changed, and he later became an active consultant on behavioral economics. It took academic work by psychologists and their publication in *Econometrica* to make an impact.[13]

The First Major Contributions

Perhaps the first notable contribution was by the psychologist George Katona, but his contribution to macroeconomic analysis, though influential in the adoption of survey analysis to project national income estimates, was essentially atheoretical and was largely ignored by academic economists. Even so, note that it correctly upended the dire predictions of most theoretically grounded economists at the end of World War II and provided the basis for the consumer research that followed.[14] Herbert Simon, an outstanding economist who also was acknowledged as a psychologist, computer scientist, and political scientist, worked primarily with economists and business administration specialists at the time of his principal contributions.[15] The latter focused on slack in the efficiency with which resources were used and the difficulty of realizing optimal results due especially to the cognitive limitations of humans. He emphasized a tendency of practitioners to employ approaches that drew on what he termed bounded rationality. (A similar emphasis was recognized later by Harvey Leibenstein.) Simon emphasized aspirations and objectives that varied from those of income maximization, and he offered satisficing as a means of attaining those objectives. (Somewhat later, Simon termed the approach of his group, procedural rationality, an alternative to the substantive rationality of mainstream economics.) Together with collaborators, Simon interviewed decision makers at length, and the results were influential, though more so with business administration specialists than with economists. Writing with the operations specialist Allen Newell, he outlined a heuristic resolution of business problems that can be regarded as a forerunner of modern behavioral economics. Nonetheless, when Simon was invited to give a talk to the American Economic Association a year before being designated as a Nobel laureate, in introducing him, Milton Friedman, the most influential American economist at the time, downplayed the seriousness of the work that Simon work was doing (and his subsequent designation as a Nobel Prize winner was contested by a number in the profession).

A major breakthrough in reintroducing psychology into formal economics came from psychologists themselves. After receiving his doctorate in psychology, Ward Edwards spent a year studying economics, and he wrote articles on decision theory that drew the attention of several prominent traditional economists. Edwards became identified with what was termed conservatism—the tendency of decision makers to incorporate new data in their calculations in a manner not consistent with Bayesian statistical rationality—but his principal contribution came through discussions in seminars concerning what was known about decision theory and with the subsequent work of his graduate students Paul Slovic, Sarah Lichtenstein, and Amos Tversky. Early on, in 1971 and 1973, Slovic and Lichtenstein showed that preferences were not necessarily stable, even in a moment of time as economic theory assumed (with the explanation why this was so, left until the 1990s in an article in the *American Economic Review*, which was written together with Tversky and Daniel Kahneman). Later in the decade, Slovic prepared an important article on the construction of preferences (still not fully accepted by economists, who, even when they deal with the matter, are more inclined to refer to a perhaps somewhat less heretical presentation by Charles Plott, one of their own).[16] Tversky combined with Kahneman to write the articles that, with the collaboration and contributions of economist Richard Thaler, led to the development of what has become modern behavioral economics and behavioral finance. Thaler has emphasized the shortcomings of traditional economic analysis as unbounded rationality, unbounded willpower, and unbounded selfishness. Major contributions to behavioral finance also were made by Robert Shiller, among others.

The most important conclusions of behavioral economics, as set out by Kahneman and Tversky, have been the emphasis on changes in wealth rather than on the overall level of wealth, and on the substantiation of loss aversion—the notion that consumers value a given amount more if it is lost than if the same amount is gained. Indeed, Dahami's overview reflects the view of behavioral economists generally in referring to loss aversion as "a fundamental trait of human nature."[17] Loss aversion was first affirmed by Adam

Smith in *The Theory of Moral Sentiments* more than two hundred years beforehand (nearly two decades before he wrote his much better-known book, *The Wealth of Nations*). The importance of changes in wealth rather than the overall level of wealth was also postulated in the mid-1950s by Markowitz, an economist who first established himself as a leader in a highly rationalist school of finance, for which he was awarded a Nobel Prize. Another truly major contribution of Kahneman and Tversky was that decisions are not made by taking probabilities into account, but by a (not completely explained) transformation of those probabilities into prospects—a human undertaking that reflects heuristics, which in turn takes account of experience, emotional considerations, and that catch-bag called intuition. In their original presentation, Kahneman and Tversky assumed that probabilities were transformed into what they termed prospects, with gains and losses calculated from the reference point of the status quo, though later investigators made several other assumptions with respect to the appropriate reference points as well. Most important is that the process of transforming probabilities into prospects usually leads to a different weighting of high and low probabilities, presumably reflecting utility, as well as more esoteric-weighting judgments. In any event, human judgment seems to vary more from objective probability near the extremes than in midpoints. Kakneman and Tversky subsequently modified their presentation to allow for the simultaneous incorporation of multiple prospects (in an approach which they termed cumulative prospect theory).

Beyond Prospect Theory

Psychologists have made many other contributions. Among them have been the tendency of most individuals to seek data that confirm their initial findings rather than to look for any negation of those findings; the tendency to affirm association with what is familiar rather than with larger categories that might include the more familiar (the conjunction bias, famous initially as the Linda phenomenon, in which the protagonist is identified by most observers as a feminist banker rather than merely as a banker); a "law of small numbers," by which we often attribute to small samples the established statistical properties of larger ones; a failure to take account of regression to the mean (still quite prominent in sports); a failure to recognize the general superiority of formulae prepared by experts to subsequent, less scientific assessments by those same experts; and the often activity-increasing but generally irrational bias of overconfidence (frequently associated with an illusion of control, though partially offset by situations of an unwarranted lack of confidence, which also leads to results different than what rational statistical calculation would indicate). An observation of psychology—mainly of Kahneman and his collaborators—that has received less support from economists is the probable difference between experienced and anticipated utility, as well as the selective role of memory in the often biased explanation of what has been experienced. Increasingly, though, it has been economists and those in finance who have contributed the most to the recent development of behavioral economics.

A number of other empirical findings have characterized behavioral economics. Often we humans make decisions as if sunk costs really do matter—for example, in continuing to use theater tickets and tennis club memberships in clearly more adverse situations than originally intended simply because we have already purchased them. Indeed, sunk costs even have played a role in major political decisions. It has been shown that differences in risk preference can occur at the same time, depending on the composition of one's endowment and the indicated reference point (which may be expected income or various other considerations, as well as Kahneman and Tversky's original status quo assumption), and also depending on whether losses from that reference point might be anticipated. In addition, there is a so-called endowment effect for goods not ordinarily traded for those that hold them, and it explains that contrary to the traditional exposition of economists, a gap between the prices sellers are willing to receive and those which buyers are willing to pay may prevent (or impede) a trade for many individuals (the notion of a market equilibrium notwithstanding). Diminishing sensitivity is a factor shown to be taken into account, both for gains and losses. The framing of data is important in human decision-making, both for the way in which individual pieces of information are presented and the manner in which they are characterized, as well as for whether that characterization contributes to a broad or to a narrow, myopic view. That has long been recognized by successful trial lawyers and marketing specialists. The overvaluation of certainty may be one of the reflections of this. Decisions about windfall gains are not dealt with in the same way as those in which components of income are earned, even though there is no difference in the dollars with which they are valued. This is one of the consequences of what happens when mental accounting, a very human inclination that reflects institutions and societal constraints and tends to ignore the fungibility of money, replaces careful calculation. Finally, procrastination, which is usually irrational, seems to be a common human phenomenon, particularly among consumers.

Subsequent Contributions

Most people's decisions have been shown to reflect a conservative status quo bias, the selection of known options similar to those that have proven successful for others, or that the decision makers have taken and are familiar with. Note, for example, that frequent experience in making certain decisions often generates a tendency for making a decision in the same manner, irrespective of the success of previous undertakings. Beyond that, decisions are sometimes made on the basis of data that is only partially relevant or indeed may not even have anything to do with the matter at hand, but that may be presented in a particularly attractive (or very forceful) manner, or that may be associated with what are viewed as particularly positive or negative factors (as in the case of cancer and certain other diseases). Decisions often differ according to whether or not people have recently been involved in extensive decision-making (though whereas two or three recent decisions of a similar type may help, a dozen or so during a short period may tax reasoning processes excessively and lead to mistaken decisions, experts in that field have assured us). Decisions also may be affected by the decision maker's general mood and state of mind, as well as the capability for making good decisions about the matter at issue. A "winner's curse" has been recognized (first identified by engineers quite independent of behavioral economics), whereby even interested and presumably knowledgeable individuals and companies pay what can only be regarded as too much at auctions (or paid too much for long periods in the past).

Originally, Kahneman and Tversky attributed such deviations from traditional economic rationality—biases in their terminology—as frequently due to the use of at least one of three heuristics (rules of thumb or shortcuts to full reasoning processes): representativeness, availability, and anchoring and adjustment. Additional general heuristics have since been cited by other social scientists. Perhaps most notable are regret (which is difficult to document and does not lead to major differences in prediction from that of the heuristics), hindsight (a tendency toward *ex post* justification, the conclusions of which also sometimes used later for *ex ante* purposes), and, recently, selection by default (particularly important in describing savings and investment choices). Emotional considerations (the affect heuristic) have received a good deal of attention, with George Loewenstein noting the distinction—and the differential impacts—between visceral (essentially physiological) factors and the impact of more volitional influences.[18] The latter usually involves beliefs and targeted groups, often playing a role in the presumably dominant cognitive heuristics and even serving to trigger (as well as inhibit) cognitive considerations.

Pattern Recognition

Pattern recognition has been cited as contributing to the ability of chess grand masters and masters in finance, along with that of presumably more mundane specialists such as firemen (as psychologist Gary Klein has documented). Here, it is necessary to distinguish between pattern recognition on the consumer side and that involving producers and investors. In any event, note that a version of pattern recognition has been claimed to be of importance for those who argue that fast and frugal heuristics may be as efficient as or even more efficient than careful calculation.

Initially, the usefulness of what Gigerenzer and his economic and psychologist associates term fast and frugal heuristics probably were applied primarily for cases in which any of several choices were likely to lead to similar results, but in reality, all heuristics are relatively fast in that they require less time to use than calculation. Moreover, other considerations also have entered that are consistent with the emphasis of the Gigerenzer followers on procedural rationality, with the effort to claim that human activity is intelligent and acts within the bounds of reason, given only the limitations of societal institutions—of being "ecologically rational."[19] However, there may be a conflict between the efficiency (the near mathematical optimality) stressed in the initial formulations of fast and frugal heuristics that do not even use all of the information available, and the possibly less efficient solutions that emerge in other, usually more complex decisions. This is acknowledged by most of those who stress a behavioral alternative to the heuristics and biases approach, which gives more credit to human intelligence and the ability of humans to come up with better solutions and to advantageously adapt the heuristics employed, even without making use of some of the available information but performing quite satisfactorily, especially after proper training.

Pattern recognition, like the other heuristics referred to, is a substitute for careful and complete calculation. One might argue that loss aversion, initially recognized as a bias, often seems to function as a heuristic, and anchoring and adjustment (a heuristic for Kahneman and Tversky) is characterized as a bias by Max Bazerman and Dan Moore in the influential *Judgment in Managerial Decision Making*.[20] Note that with the exception of Gigerenzer's fast and frugal heuristics, all those that have been noted are general heuristics; they really cry out for further definition. Incidentally, there is no unambiguous theory of heuristics, and use of some heuristics may lead to results that conflict with others. Behavioral economists have given much less attention to the specific heuristics that guide much, and perhaps most, actual decision-making.

Behavioral Finance

A breakthrough study in finance dates to 1981, when Robert Shiller, then essentially a more traditional economist, showed that the volatile movement of stock prices greatly exceeded the discounted changes in anticipated dividends, as presumably would have been the case had the movements of stock share prices been dependent strictly on rational factors. This influential study is one of a small group of analyses not based on individual behavior. Subsequent analyses revealed a disposition bias, whereby investors tended to sell stocks that had risen rapidly (termed winners) and delay the sale of stocks that had declined (termed losers) That type of action disregarded expected outcomes, as would have been indicated by then much-vaunted Efficient Market Hypothesis—and indeed, this even occurred in countries such as the United States, in which there was a tax incentive to sell losers and hold winners. It was maintained that this disposition effect was a reflection of loss aversion and several other biases. In country after country, it has been shown that it would have made sense to purchase stocks that had been losers for a number of years, and to sell those that had been winners over that period—though at first few stockbrokers dared advocate such a trading plan (at least until the introduction of an oversimplified version of that approach, known as the Dogs of the Dow). Bandwagon and other feedback effects were common in the stock market (and may help explain the extraordinary market gyrations since early February 2018). Moreover, initially a January effect was detected, whereby stocks (mainly shares in stocks of small companies) rose more at the beginning of a new year than in comparable periods during the year itself, at least for a time. The premium for owning stocks vis-à-vis bonds has been shown to far exceed any rational explanation, and this finding has generated any number of efforts to explain the same, perhaps the most convincing and behaviorally relevant being the frequency with which individuals tended to check the respective prices.

Additional Contributions

Behavioral economics has recognized that deviations from rationality are not exclusively those of properly valuing currencies. The field has grappled even more to explain problems of self-control, and although various commitment devices have been noted, it has also been observed (especially by Frank) that the nature of some outcomes that are irrational in terms of traditional economic rationality are intentional and may be quite rational in some overall perspective.[21] Addiction has been explained in part as due to underestimation of the time required to complete projects, but it also has been noted that addiction alters the chemistry of the brain. To overcome inconsistencies to rationality over time, economists have resorted to traditional, time-consistent discounting. Behavioral economists have shown that other approaches, though also somewhat arbitrary, seem to better incorporate observed human inclinations and predict better (notably, hyperbolic and quasi-hyperbolic discounting). Behavioral economics has continued to deal with the temporal distortions of decisions. Two-self models (sometimes referred to as planner and doer models) also have been introduced, though perhaps more commonly the reference is to mega and secondary preferences. These explain differences in the way in which we deal with different quantities of money, but there still does not seem to be a good theoretical explanation for people's willingness to accept negative rates of interest in some cases (e.g., schoolteachers who tend to prefer payments spread out over a year rather than for the nine months in which they usually work).

There have been many other contributions. Discounts and rebates of the same amount have been shown to be viewed differently (one being viewed as more permanent than the other) and to elicit different responses. The same dollar value of costs and benefits are frequently not held to have the same consequences (with reasoning along the lines of loss aversion). Arbitrage has been shown to be limited in its potential for eliminating discrepancies in markets. Differential responses to fairness, reciprocity, and punishment have received a great deal of attention, especially in evaluating the ultimatum and dictator games. Fairness and justice are frequently defined in terms of the social norms of given communities, contrary to what traditional economics would indicate. Similarly, the importance of what has been termed choice architecture has been emphasized. There have even been efforts to offer conclusions about happiness, although that topic is not considered legitimate by all behavioral economists.[22]

Applications

The findings of behavioral economics have led to numerous successful applications. Changes have been registered in legal systems, tending away from what had long been a noneconomic and then a mainstream rationalist approach to adopt the findings of behavioral economics. Offices (usually temporary) have been established in Great Britain, the United States, and other countries to modify laws and regulations more along behavioral lines. We have come to recognize and perhaps understand the rationale behind much that is related to consumer behavior with respect to insurance and taxes. In addition, employment of the findings of behavioral economics has succeeded in getting a greater proportion of employees to elect savings plans when first hired (thanks to use of a default heuristic that has gotten individuals to move away from a myopic approach that tended to lead to undersaving for retirement) and subsequently to save more than they would have, *at least on average* (by use of alternative form of nudging). Mind you, this has taken place in the context of what by most measures has been a decline in national savings rates. In both the private and public sectors, nudging has been used to help improve decision-making regardless of whether or not this has led to the most efficient or most desired solution possible or whether it is even the best use of the findings of behavioral economics. Moreover, the nudging literature has come to recognize the importance of nonfinancial incentives—though here too, there is an issue of valuing or ranking the various incentives.[23] Perhaps the most dramatic application of the principles of behavioral economics (along with those of applied mathematics) has been in the improvement in the allocation of organ transplants.

There is a good deal of work still in progress. Strategic interaction appears to be dependent on behavioral game theory, and although the latter has been achieving more plausible results, it is rarely based on more than the isolated observed behavior of individuals and almost never on overall patterns of strategic interaction.[24] Finally, strategic analysis cries out for a psychologically more acceptable explanation of learning than that which has been employed. (Only psychologists seemed to be concerned with this. Simon was one, but his work in this field, done together with other psychologists, continues to be overlooked.) Finally, neuroeconomics may underlie all of the findings of behavioral economics, but it remains to be more fully explained, and the costs of altering basic physiological tendencies are unclear.

Texts in Behavioral Economics

Among the most popular texts in behavioral economics have been Bazerman's (now Bazerman and Moore's) *Judgment in Managerial Decision Making* and Dan Ariely's *Predictably Irrational and the Hidden Forces that Shape Our Decisions.*[25] The Bazerman volume is considered in chapter 3 because, after a presentation of the most common findings of behavioral economics, it indicates how decision makers (in this case, managerial decision makers) might endeavor to make their decisions. Ariely's entertaining and revealing contribution has focused mainly on consumers. He reports on experiments that reveal human behavior to be just as other behavioral economics experiments have shown, which he terms irrational but also quite predictable. It's a great read, and the point on the predictability of results certainly comes through, but his approach would appear to neglect several points.

First, it doesn't consider whether some of those "irrational" results may in fact be rational in terms of a more global rationality, considering noneconomic factors (whether some of the "irrationalities" might not have been intended). Perhaps that is consistent with Ariely's stress of the importance of emotions and relativity concerns, though. Second, the approach doesn't attempt to estimate the cost of the irrationalities. And, third, it does not ask whether we can eliminate or at least reduce those irrationalities, and if so, which offer the most promising prospects. That's true, though toward the end of his presentation, the author notes that the irrationality is due in part to limitations in the perception of information (which can be reduced by dedicating more attention to improving perception) and to social norms (which can be reduced by changes in those norms, or which can be eliminated or reduced by what has become known as nudging). He does not consider what the cost of such efforts might be and thus whether the efforts might be worthwhile or, given the variance in consumer behavior, likely to be much greater for some activities than others of consequence for decision-making. Neither does he consider whether a society should favor those with the more rational responses, at least in some activities. And Ariely's presentation, in *Predictably Irrational* as elsewhere, has focused overwhelmingly on consumer decision-making and on the options made available to individual consumers—*given* producer decisions, that is—or on the possibly very different and sometimes presumably more traditional nature of decision-making for producers (as well as on the less financially maximizing decisions of institutional organizations).

Unresolved Concerns

Application of the empirical findings of behavioral economics has achieved a great deal but did little to help extract us from the 2008–2012 greatest recession in modern times or even to move corporations and other organizations in a desired direction. A reason for this, in addition to the relatively slow advance of behavioral macroeconomics, may be that although it has become clearer that actual economic behavior (descriptive economics) reflects psychological considerations and other-than-mathematical human frailties, it has overlooked the fact that there are extraordinary differences in the behavior of individuals and the behavior of a society that is determined by the major role of one or few individuals in a large and perhaps increasing number of the organizations that in turn reflect a large and increasing share of the value of its activities.

The list of economic anomalies, irrationalities, is much longer than what is indicated here. It is clear that behavioral economics has had an impact on what takes place in society. Nonetheless, although some of the seemingly irrational consumer phenomena have dissipated over time, particularly as their presumed irrationalities were publicized, others have not, and for the most part, behavioral economists have failed to explain (indeed, by and large, have not even attempted to explain) the reasons for this. It's similar for the mixed results of an increased incidence of the generally predictable but, as seen for the long term, irrational phenomena for changes in degree of competition. Why does competition seem to have such a demonstrable effect in eliminating what seemed to be irrationality in some cases and not in others? Neither has there been much attention to the differential impact of these irrationalities on different activities, nor to the differential cost of alleviating them, particularly in relation to the cost that the irrationalities inflicted. More important for the argument of this presentation, though it has been obvious in some of the studies, there is tremendous variation between individuals and organizations in the degree to which these phenomena, irrational from a traditional point of view, have inflicted a cost[26] or in the degree to which the deviations from what we have termed rationality have prevailed over time, as well as in the short run. The money illusion, the tendency to fail to adequately recognize the impact of low rates of inflation on a constant value of money, appears to have persisted despite centuries of experience and numerous writings on the subject, suggesting that some biases persist in the long and the short run.

CHAPTER 3

The Guidelines for Producer and Other Organizational Decision Makers

Only since the end of World War II does there seem to have been much interest in formulating guidelines for decision makers. In the mid-1940s, Simon submitted his doctoral dissertation (in political science), which was published in 1947 as *Administrative Behavior: A study of decision-making processes in administrative organizations.*[27] A number of guidelines appeared after that, and this chapter will refer to several of them, notably texts for business administration students. What is perhaps even more notable than the current emphasis on the failure of many consumers to follow the principles of economic optimality is the inclination of the guidelines to use evidence based largely on consumer behavior to suggest what was desirable for organizations. (Popular commentators continued to offer advice for consumers, of course, particularly in daily newspapers, and many of the latter incorporated the same guidelines that were being given to corporations, though they actually were more relevant for consumers.) The same inclination with respect to the use of guidelines for organizations largely holds for Simon's subsequent work related to economics at the Carnegie Institute for Technology (subsequently Carnegie-Mellon University). Several other notable considerations also were missing in all of these guidelines, as will be noted at the end of the chapter.

First, Simon's guidelines. *Administrative Behavior* began with chapters on decision-making and administrative organization and on administrative theory, continued with chapters on what Simon termed fact and value in decision-making and on the rationality in administrative behavior, and concluded with chapters on the psychology of administrative decisions, the equilibrium of the organization, the rule of authority, communication, the criterion of efficiency, loyalties, and the anatomy of organization.

Even as he added comments over the years reflecting advances in the professional literature, and as much as he was also a psychologist (the department with which Simon was most identified with in the last decades of his life), his comments did not make explicit reference to the work of Kahneman and Tversky and the other leading behavioral decision theorists, although he regarded their work on heuristics as a logical follow-up to his own. The various editions of *Administrative Behavior* coincide with his emphasis on procedural rationality, but they are relatively open with respect to precisely what steps organizations should take. It is not that Simon was entirely an academic; he spent more than a year with a municipality and was a member of the first US aid agency. Rather, he concluded that given the differences confronting organizations and the differences in the organizations themselves, the implementation of the principles he laid down did not lend themselves to exactly the same measures for all organizations. The analysis of those chapters and the comments that followed would have been quite useful for those organizations that would have taken the trouble to read them and follow up on the advice given. The major qualification, perhaps, would be with respect to what was characterized as learning, about which Simon, the psychologist, was involved in studies late in life that led him to differ from what the behavioral economics community has assumed and continues to assume about the subject: that learning can be gauged entirely from the results of the experiments that economists have conducted with alternative incentives.[28]

This analysis considers half a dozen recent books and provides comments on four that have been used to convey the principles of organizational decision-making, along with articles in the 2014–2017 issues of both the *Journal of Behavioral Decision Making* and *Judgment and Decision Making*.

A frequently revised, primarily undergraduate college text, Jerald Greenberg's *Behavior in Organizations* contains a chapter on decision-making that covers most of the principal topics. Its presentation is relatively straightforward with respect to the emerging literature of behavioral economics. The book is divided into sections dealing with formulation, consideration, and implementation.

A somewhat more sophisticated text by Josef Maria Rosanas, a professor at the IESE Business School, is *Decision Making in an Organizational Context*, was published in 2013.[29] It handles the difficult matter of interpersonal relations by dealing first with "personal decisions where other people are far away," and only afterward with "personal decisions where other people are near." The book devotes space to the subject of learning early on, but it does not enter explicitly into the underlying psychological explanations. It deals with transaction analysis, incomplete contracts and informal organizations, stakeholders and shareholders, motives, and the issue of corporate social responsibility. It has a section specifically on decisions within an organization.

The Oxford Handbook of Organizational Decision Making, edited by Gerald P. Hodgkinson and William H. Starbuck, was published in 2008.[30] Several chapters are especially relevant to this book, but most notable is Zur Shapira's "On the Implications of Behavioral

Decision Making." Most of that chapter covers the material referred to here in chapter 2, but of note is a section dealing with ambiguity, and another that gives attention to what psychologists have termed the inside-outside view. There is a section on alternative notions of rationality as well. The volume also contains chapters on intuition in organizational decision-making, affect and information processing, and (seemingly close to the focus of this presentation) individual differences and decision-making.

Of interest too is Joseph E. Champoux's *Organizational Behavior: Integrating Individuals, Groups and Organizations,* the fifth edition of which was published in 2017.[31] Chapter 14, "Decision Making and Problem Solving," contains sections on decision strategies, decision-making processes, and decision-making models (which deals with a rational model and a bounded rationality model). There is also a discussion of choosing between individual and group decision-making. The chapter closes with a section on improving decision-making that includes what it terms human-based methods (brainstorming, the Delphi method, what is termed a devil's advocate approach, and dialectical inquiry) as well as computer-based methods. The section on choosing between individual and group decision-making does not deal with the issues raised in this book.

Finally, perhaps the most useful book is the latest rendition of *Judgment in Managerial Decision Making, Eighth Edition* by Max H. Bazerman and Don A. Moore (Hoboken, NJ: Wiley, 2013). The first eight chapters review (and reorder) what the academic studies of individuals have shown about behavioral decision-making, categorizing them basically as involving bounded willpower, bounded self-interest, bounded awareness, and bounded ethicality.

Chapter 2, "Overconfidence," is indicated to facilitate many of the other biases (with sections on overprecision, overestimation and overplacement; experts; blindness to biases; overestimation, self-enhancement, illusion of control, the planning fallacy, and what is termed overplacement). Chapter 3, "Common Biases," deals with the use of past decision processes for future problems, biases emanating from the availability heuristic (ease of recall/vividness; retrievability based on memory structures); biases emanating from the representative heuristic (insensitivity to base rates and sample size; misconception of chance; regression to the mean; the conjunction fallacy); and biases emanating from the confirmation heuristic (anchoring; conjunctive and disconjunctive events bias; hindsight and the curse of knowledge).

Chapter 4, "Bounded Awareness/Availability," covers intentional blindness, change blindness, focalism and the focusing illusion, bounded awareness in groups, and bounded awareness in strategic settings and auctions (the winner's curse). Chapter 5, "Framing and the Reversal of Preferences," discusses certainty, the underweighting of merely high probability items, framing and the overselling of insurance, rebate and bonus framing, and joint versus separate preference reversals). Chapter 6, "Motivational and Emotional Influences on Decision Making," tackles multiple selves, temporal differences, reconciling internal conflicts, and self-serving reasoning. Chapter 7, "The Estimation of Commitment," covers perceptual biases, judgmental biases, impression management, and competitive irrationality. Chapter 8 is entitled "Fairness and Ethics in Decision-Making."

So far, there is no major deviation from what I would characterize as a not entirely unreasonable application of the findings based on experiments with individuals to business organizations. That begins to change in the remainder of the Bazerman and Moore book, however.

The remaining chapters deal with ways in which managers can improve organizational decision-making and seem more consistent with the apparent behavior of the three successful business executives considered in chapter 5 of this book. Indeed, one cannot help but wonder if the decision-making behavior of those individuals might better have been taken as a basis for principles of decision-making in business rather than the results of experiments with consumers.

Chapter 9 outlines common investment mistakes. Chapters 10 and 11 explain rational decision-making in negotiations. Finally, chapter 12, "Improving Decision-Making," outlines seven strategies (notably, debias your judgment, reason analogically, take an outsider's view, understand the biases of others, nudge more wisely and make more ethical decisions). These strategies extend the guidance well beyond that offered by the findings of behavioral economics, and to an extent, they appear to be consistent with the considerations of behavioral game theory.

What is most striking is that none of the advisory texts deal with the *range* of decisions that individuals and organizations make—some of which are near what is most sought by government policy, and some of which are distant from that—along with the implications that this presents for government policy. Moreover, although there is some discussion of the ways to increase the receptivity of middle and lower-level functionaries to corporate decisions, and there is limited discussion of a kind of altruism (noted by Simon, in any event). There is no recognition of the fact that most major organizational decisions are made by one or few individuals, and it would appear that the organizations for which this is most true have come to constitute a larger part of the economy in recent years. More important, no guidance is provided on how to get more knowledgeable senior employees below the level of the major decision makers to implement the decisions of the major decision makers—or how the major decision makers should respond to the implementation of those senior employees. Implementation is overlooked (which is perhaps to be expected from most of those who have not been involved in actual operations). In addition to everything else, it is unclear that the major decision makers make their decisions along the lines that decision-making guidelines recommend, and in fact, it is unlikely that they do so for several reasons, but in part because their reasoning involves more individuals and usually is more dynamic than what is indicated by most decision-making guidelines. This will be made clearer in chapters 5 and 6.

Examination of articles in the *Journal of Behavioral Decision Making* and *Judgment and Decision Making* for the years 2014–2017 does not reveal any significant differences from the guidelines in the texts cited. Moreover, I perused the titles of articles in the *Journal of Economic Behavior and Organization* for the years 2014–2017, and none deal with the decision-making process in corporations. Only one in the *Journal of Business Research* did—only a single article in four years. Although that article focuses on the decision-making in a firm, the enterprise is quite small and is far from dominant in its industry.

CHAPTER 4

Movement toward What Is Required—the Interview-Based Studies

The interview-based studies, as undertaken to date, reflect movement between the laboratory studies and what a behavioral analysis truly requires. Initially their intention was more ambitious. The first interview-based studies, directed at industrial corporations and primarily at key individuals in those corporations, aimed at understanding the way in which decisions were made, if not generally then in the industrial sector or in the relevant branch of the sector. The studies accomplished this by obtaining responses from CEOs and other leaders explaining why their companies made the decisions that they did. What follows is a chapter longer than the others, detailing the findings of interview-based studies in an attempt to capture the role of those studies in moving toward what behavioral economics requires in order to achieve the goal set out decades before, that of reflecting the mixed behavioral assumptions of the decision-making of all entities. The reader might find it useful to regard the chapter as divided in two: my effort to cover a relatively wide base of producer decision-making, and an alternative endeavor to more thoroughly examine an even larger number of producers in a narrower base.

Laboratory experiments are based on decisions that are revealed, though in a hypothetical setting. Individuals are involved, and although they vary in their responses, the findings of the experiments focus on average results. Implicitly, outliers are treated as black swans (aided over time by a persuasive book with a title along those lines), though that approach appears to be mistaken, seriously limiting interpretation of the results. Enterprises with responses reflecting an absence of at least some of the behavioral biases might well be expected to emerge as particularly successful, even dominant enterprises. Indeed, that appears to have been precisely what happened in the case of most of the enterprises of Steve Jobs, Elon Musk, and Jeff Bezos. This important fact appears to have been overlooked by the laboratory experimenters. The results of the field or natural experiments are also based on actual decisions, though in a limited set of circumstances, and again, they are focused on overall results—on average results—ignoring the often significant differences in individual responses. Again, as in the case of the laboratory experiments, some of the outlying responses undoubtedly reflect an absence of certain behavioral biases and should not be ignored—as most of the field studies also do.

The interview-based studies gathered a large amount of information, with the aim of helping to understand the responses volunteered that indicated why specific decisions were made. Some of the results ran counter to those indicated in the laboratory and field exercises. That should have been helpful, both in isolating outliers (particularly those with a lack of at least several behavioral biases) and in understanding a decision-making process that probably involved more than one individual and may have shifted over time. Undoubtedly, much also depended on the familiarity of the interviewer with the industry or type of situation in question, and his or her skill in eliciting good responses; to this should be added the objectivity of the interviewer, or at least the willingness of the interviewer to reveal his or her biases and the ability of readers to take those biases into account. In any event, the interview-based studies also erred or missed an opportunity in usually attempting to suggest industry-wide, or at least individual industry behavior rather than in singling out the nature of decision-making of those industrialists who did not show as many behavioral biases and thus tended to triumph over those that did—and whose decision-making was less like that of consumers whose well-documented behavior constituted the basis of so much of the advice given to producers and other organizations about optimal decision-making behavior.

Unfortunately, the sometimes contrary interview-based results do not appear to have influenced most in the behavioral economics community, and it does not even seem that they had the most desirable effect on those conducting the studies. The interview-based approach has seldom been used in economics, and generally it has been rejected as too time-consuming and too unscientific—though that criticism has been strongly refuted by the most prominent of the interviewers, an economist whose methodological credentials are well established.[32] (The article defending interview data as a valid empirical tool has been largely ignored, perhaps because of the fact that it appeared in a less well-known journal.)

Of the now numerous economists, psychologists, and others who became involved in behavioral analyses, very few have attempted to conduct interviews aimed at ferreting out why the entities made the decisions they did, and even fewer have succeeded in publishing their results. Moreover, not all of the behavioral work has been published, and indeed, it is possible that the most important interview-based studies have not yet made it into print for one reason or another.

I am one of those authors. I have a PhD in economics (Yale) and was specialized initially in industrial economics. I taught, worked in an international agency, and consulted. I am fairly well regarded but not prominent. I have lived in several countries, fluently speak the languages in which the interviews were conducted, and consulted with experts concerning interviewing techniques to a limited degree. At present, I consider myself to be a behavioral economist. My work has only occasionally been cited.

The second author, Truman Bewley, holds PhDs in economics and mathematics from the University of California at Berkeley, and he is known primarily as an expert in general equilibrium theory. He has been involved primarily as an academic at Yale University and is regarded as an expert in his primary field. He has lived in at least two countries and is a native speaker of the language in which the interviews were conducted. Bewley does not consider himself a behavioral economist, and though he is personally well regarded by the leaders in the behavioral economics community, his work in that field has been cited principally for its contribution to one of the issues with which he has dealt, fairness. It is only for that finding that he appears to have any prominent followers among behavioral economists. Bewley's principal work in behavioral economics has drawn praise from a number of labor economists and several other leading economists who are not behavioral economists; his work in his principal field, general equilibrium economics, is well regarded.

The third author is Philip Bromiley, a professor of business administration long associated with the University of Minnesota; he is currently at the University of California, Irvine. His PhD is from Carnegie Mellon, where his dissertation committee was headed by Herbert Simon. Bromiley describes himself as a consultant in behavioral risk management and has advised many corporations and other organizations. His recent publications deal with business administration, as well as behavioral economics.

The fourth author is Alan Blinder of Princeton and New York University, who received his PhD from Princeton. Blinder was vice chairman of the Federal Reserve Board. He is a monetary and macroeconomic specialist who's very well regarded in that field, though he's not considered a member of the behavioral economics community and has not been active recently in behavioral publications.

Only a small number of interview-based studies have been published. By far the most important is Bewley's book *Why Wages Don't Fall During a Recession,* based on data from 1990–1991, mainly from approximately three hundred New England manufacturers and associated persons. It was published in 1999[33] following several articles on the interviews in the 1990s. He has been working on a further study involving an even larger number of interviews, but that is still being revised, having been delayed by Bewley's work in his principal area of expertise, his administrative obligations, and perhaps other considerations.

This writer authored four interview-based studies: an article published in 1987 and based on data from 113 US, Mexican, and Argentine manufacturers gathered in 1976–1977; an appendix to a book published in 1998, based on 36 Uruguayan manufacturing companies; a report based on largely monthly data collected in 2003 for a dozen Fortune 1000 companies, published in 2004; and a chapter combining the aforementioned results in a volume edited by Morris Altman in 2006.[34] Those studies have been combined with a further report involving smaller companies, but that report was not accepted for publication by two journals that ordinarily have been receptive to manuscripts on behavioral economics.

In addition, there are a few more publications based on interviews. Bromiley published a book in 1986, and though he has been in frequent contact with corporations and other entities, his recent publications have not made mention of interviews. Blinder published a study in 1998 on the price stickiness of companies, together with several other authors, but he has not been involved in interview-based studies since.[35] The response of most economic and business analysts has been to ignore most of these efforts; there have been a number of reviews of Bewley (1999), however, as well as summaries of the book published in other works, or rather, chiefly of the portion dealing with the fairness issue. The most common response of economists appears to be to claim (privately) that such studies are unscientific and take too long, and to ignore whether they make a contribution to understanding economic behavior.

The Published Bewley Studies

Truman Bewley, a general equilibrium theorist, became concerned with the behavioral assumptions of the traditional economic models with which he had to work. For that reason, he set off to interview 336 business leaders, union officials, employment counselors, and related professionals in the New England region to inquire into wage decisions made during the relatively short US economic recession of 1990–1991. His basic goal was to uncover better micro assumptions for macro analysis, a major area in which behavioral economics had made few inroads (and still has not done so).

This account is taken largely from pages 363–368 of my chapter "Interviews as a Means of Understanding Economic Reasoning" in Altman's *Handbook of Contemporary Behavioral Economics*. A summary of the findings prepared for this publication follows.

Bewley (1999) has four objectives, three of which are dealt with here. Most important, he offers the results of interviews dealing with wage rigidity and a host of factors regarding employment — company risk aversion, internal and external pay structure, hiring generally, and the pay of hires in what he terms the primary and secondary sectors, in particular raises, resistance to pay reduction, layoffs, severance benefits, voluntary turnover, the situation of the unemployed, labor negotiation, and (directly and indirectly) morale. He maintains that it is necessary to understand the mechanisms creating unemployment because that is critical for discovering how to reduce it. Second, the book offers arguments for and against the type of less structured, open-ended approach of basically listening to firms with only a memorized list of questions and concerns, not all of which are to be asked of all of those interviewed. The overall study introduced the results of many statistical analyses to help assess the interview findings. Third, the book provides a careful description (as well as a critique) of the leading theories that have been advanced to explain wage rigidity, and it evaluates those theories in the light of the evidence of the respondents and other evidence more generally available.

The conclusion is that only one theoretical explanation seems to be consistent with the evidence uncovered: that dealing with the importance of morale. The other theories lead to conclusions that are not supported by the evidence, and he attributes this shortcoming to their reliance on unrealistic assumptions about employer (and employee) behavior. The analysis then attempts to deal with the rather imprecise concept that is morale. Finally, Bewley (1999) offers suggestions on what might be done next. This includes the use of additional surveys and tests of existing theories and his reinforced theory of wage rigidity.

Bewely states that his interview findings support only those economic theories of wage rigidity that emphasize the impact of pay cuts on morale. He points to the models of Solow (1979), Akerlof (1982), and Akerlof and Yellen (1988, 1990).

Bewley discusses problems with surveys. He observes that motives may be unconscious—people may not be aware of the principles governing their behavior—and he cites implicit contracting as an example of this. He comments that in the course of the study, he learned that cutting pay would have almost no effect on employment, that hiring new workers at reduced pay would antagonize them, that reducing the pay of existing workers would affect worker attitudes, and that the advantage of layoffs over pay cuts is that it gets misery out of the door. None of the employers he spoke with stated that they offered a choice between layoffs and lower pay. The interviews revealed that labor is in excess supply during recessions, that employers avoid hiring overqualified workers, and that to the extent there is some downward wage flexibility, it is in secondary markets that are characterized by heavy turnover and relatively more part-time work.

The initial interviews were arranged through the New Haven Chamber of Commerce and personal connections, but the majority came through references from those sources and from cold calls. Bewley aimed for a varied sample but looked particularly for companies that had experienced large layoffs. He changed the focus of the interviews over time, moving from an initial emphasis on wage and salary structures to a greater emphasis on questions of morale and overqualification. He undertook all of the interviews personally and made some telephone follow-ups. He concluded that the sessions with a fixed list of questions were less successful than those that were more free-flowing. The focus was on the experience of the companies interviewed, and his questions avoided economic jargon, with any theoretical queries reserved for the end of the sessions. He emphasized factual matters and did not ask direct questions about interpretive issues. Whereas Blinder and colleagues (1998) interviewed only sellers of goods and services, Bewley spoke with buyers as well, and he did not attempt to avoid discussions that might be considered to be frightening (such as those bearing in collusion), as the Blinder study did. He did avoid gathering precise quantitative data, however.

Bewley found that managers believed morale to be vital for productivity, recruitment, and retention. He defined good morale as characterized by a common sense of purpose consistent with company goals (not unlike what Simon 1990, 1992, and 1993 referred to as a variant of altruism—selfish altruism, in Simon's terms), cooperativeness, happiness or tolerance of unhappiness, zest for the job, moral behavior, mutual trust, and ease of communication (p. 41). In discussing what affects morale, he noted a sense of community, an understanding of company actions and policies, and a belief that company actions are fair, along with an employee's emotional state, ego satisfaction from work, and trust in coworkers and in company leadership. His respondents indicated that poor morale led to low productivity, poor customer service, high turnover, and recruiting difficulties. There is no specification of any trade-offs that might be involved in the role of the various factors in contributing to morale, in the precise impact of morale on productivity, or in the precise role of that morale-based productivity in keeping wages relatively rigid.

A chapter on company risk aversion contributes to the discussion, as do the chapters on the external and internal pay structure, the latter of which is held to be important to internal harmony and morale, job performance, and turnover. The results indicate that the rigidity of new hires in the primary sector stems from considerations about the internal pay structure. The findings on salary increases reveal that beyond what is required by contracts, managers view raises as important in providing incentives and motivation. They are driven by the same factors in recession as in good times, he found: profits, the cost of living, raises in other firms, product market competition, and the competition for labor. Raises are not delayed because of concern about turnover of key employees. Managers resist reducing pay during a recession for fear of its effect on morale and the effect of that on productivity, along with concern for turnover of the best employees—these factors are much more important than any pressure from labor unions.

Layoffs are preferred to pay cuts not only because the latter are felt to affect the morale and productivity of the remaining workforce more, but also because labor costs were estimated to be a small part of total costs (and so would facilitate only small reductions in prices), and demand was often held to be relatively inelastic. Layoffs also were preferred to pay cuts where it was not felt that competitors would match price cuts, or where competition was based on more than price. Layoffs were favored as well where it was concluded that sales levels were lower because of financial difficulties of the firms involved (in which case, demand for the firm in question would not be helped much by wage reductions because of the level of benefits also available to employees), because of considerations of technological change, because of the opportunity to reorganize operations and eliminate organizational slack, and because of the possibility of increasing the work of the remaining employees. Bewley found that most severance pay obligations were not high (because it was believed that there was a lack of employee interest in them). It was uncommon to replace employees with cheaper labor because it was felt that the company would lose in terms of skill and morale. Managers acknowledged that those laid off were dealt a heavy blow, but they concluded that the psychological impact did not extend to the rest of the workforce.

Interviews with labor officials indicated that the information asymmetries assumed in some theoretical explanations of wage rigidity were not of much significance. Similarly, the shirking theory, which assumes that workers are paid more than necessary and are dismissed if they do not meet certain standards, was rejected as an explanation of wage rigidity, as were all efficiency wage theories.

The principal critique of the existing theories is given in chapter 20 of Bewley (1999).

Finally, Bewley presents his extension of a morale-based theory of wage rigidity. Before doing so, he states:

> Crucial aspects of the theory are that productivity depends on employees' mood that workers with good morale internalize their firm's goals, and that pay cuts impair both mood and identification with the employer. None of these aspects is closely connected with rationality, which, in economists' usage, has to

> do with striving to achieve given objectives rather
> than with the selection of objectives or with the
> psychological capacity to accomplish them, matters
> central to morale. Nor does there seem to be a useful
> way to discuss formally the choice of objectives. I
> propose … a choice theoretic theory of mood that
> does not glaringly conflict with rationality. (p. 430)

Bewley adds, "I believe it is a general human experience that capacities to act and perceptions of pain or pleasure adapt to our circumstances" (p. 443). He then presents a model that "preserves the utility maximization principle used in economics." That model includes unconsciously and consciously felt mental and physical goals and costs.

There seems to be a point at which wage rigidity does break down, and the seeds of that breakdown are captured in some of the responses Bewley notes.

Bewley characterizes the information gathered from interviews as uncovering motives, constraints, and an understanding of the decision-making process. He acknowledges the uncertain reliability of some interview responses (and indicates efforts to detect and deal with inconsistencies), but one might hope that his current study of prices would specify how much time passed between the events and the recording of information that took place in those events.

To sum up, Bewley relied on open-ended, in-depth interviews, listening to the replies (sometimes extended) of those being interviewed and concentrating on those replies that dealt with actual entrepreneurial experiences. Later, in analyzing his findings, his book takes account of a large number of relevant works in economic theory and econometrics. His major conclusion is that morale—defined to include both consciously and unconsciously felt mental and physical goals and costs—influences productivity and in turn profitability. He maintains that except for those cases in which there are severe impacts in the financial condition of individual enterprises that is obvious to employees, or in which there are pronounced declines in the overall economy, morale is affected more by wage reductions than by personnel layoffs. Basically, he surmised that the adversity in the latter case lies primarily outside the workplace, whereas in the former, the adversity is felt directly by those in the plant. Bewley summarized his analysis in chapters in two books, and several prominent economists reflected on the possible importance of his approach in understanding economic behavior generally. However, no one seems to have followed his example of interviewing decision makers.

A few economists had published articles that assumed that the morale of those on the job might be adversely affected by wage cuts (notably Akerlof), though without any indication as to how their morale might be affected if their wages had not been reduced but other workers in the same plant had been laid off. It is difficult to imagine how meaningful insights such as those concerning the differential impact on the morale of workers under those alternative situations could be obtained in highly controlled laboratory experiments with students if the usually youthful and inexperienced participants had been asked to respond in a manner that would have captured responses as if they had been long employed and had become dependent on their wages for the well-being of their families. (Neither have there been experiments in which the participants, also confronted with the two types of situations, were carried out in comparably adverse or even more normal times.) Relevant to the thesis of the presentation of this book is the question of whether there were some cases in which the CEO—some Jeff Bezos, perhaps—or some other member of management devised approaches that avoided an adverse impact on the morale of those employees still on the job when other workers were laid off, though such a finding would not be inconsistent with Bewley's overall results.

As far as I am aware, there has only been a single laboratory experiment that has dealt with the Bewley findings, at least partially upholding the latter's emphasis of morale on productivity and profitability: a draft submitted to SSRN in August 2017—nearly two decades after publication of Bewley (1999) and more than two decades after the initial publication of the results in articles. To be fair, another by several prominent laboratory researchers may still be awaiting publication.

Bewley came to several conclusions that might be verified in the laboratory, but as far as I am aware, there have not been any other studies, despite the widespread circulation of his findings and the numerous experiments undertaken since those findings were published. Presumably this reflects a bias against encouraging interview-based studies, and perhaps a concern that some of the latter may upend available laboratory results. In any event, it should be noted that Bewley found, for example, that labor unions did not seem to be particularly concerned with severance pay (at least, not during relatively short downturns such as the one he studied). This would appear to counter a good deal of received knowledge and might be examined further. Another result of the interviews was that informational asymmetries do not seem to explain relative wage rigidity, despite the importance that the latter have been given in some major theories of labor economics. (Perhaps the authors of those theories should revise the theories if they have not already done so. The finding might well hold, even if wage rigidities do not apply to some companies in which one or few persons determine the decisions.) Beyond that, do Bewley's findings, if corroborated, have policy implications (particularly along the lines of the presentation of this book) if the rigidities do not hold for some of those companies in which one or few persons determine decisions? There would then seem to be other policy implications as well. Indeed, perhaps the major limitation of the Bewley (1999) study is that it ignores the consequences of the producer response of outliers.

Bewley presents a strong case for the validity of empirical data drawn from open-ended, in-depth interviews (in Bewley 2002), which was prepared as he was beginning to prepare drafts of his study on price formation in which he interviewed approximately six hundred firms. "An obvious way to learn about motives, constraints, and the decision making processes is to ask decision makers about them," Bewley begins (p. 343). "Whatever the method of sampling, he adds, it is vital … to achieve as much variety as possible … because without it you cannot see the connections between responses and the circumstances of various types of respondents" (p. 345). The affirmation is an argument for the type of study advocated in this book's presentation, particularly given the importance of the way in which organizational decision-making proceeds, but unfortunately there has not been any corresponding follow-up. On the contrary, Bewley follows a theme common among modern economists, maintaining, "If the objective is to understand the shape of a general phenomenon with a view to formulating new theories, then the style should be less structured in the hopes that the respondent will come up with unexpected descriptions and arguments" (p. 346).

Bewley concludes that although systematically following a fixed list of questions (the most usual approach in survey analyses) leads to fewer inconsistencies and contradictions, to a degree, a less structured approach could offset the possible disadvantage in that respect by broaching important issues at several separated times and in different ways. He maintained that use of a looser, more relaxed discussion "was more consistent with the overall logic of their remarks and probably reflected their views more accurately" (p. 346).

"The main questions have to do with the person's decision problem; its objectives, the possible actions, the constraints on them, the decisions made, how they are arrived at, and how they change with circumstance," Bewely continues (p. 347). "The most you can hope for … is to see a coherent story of the interaction of motivation and constraints that leads to decisions" (pp. 348–349).

One should not accept what people say about their actions at face value, Bewley acknowledges, and he suggests that actions should be observed if it is possible to do so. With respect to the view that interview data should not be trusted because this leads to an emphasis on irrational behavior, whereas rationality is the common thread that holds economic theory (and much human action) together, Bewley observes that "interviewing reveals rationality as well as irrationality" (p. 350). Behavioral economists, who have shown the frequency and yet general predictability of irrationality, might be more in line with what we know if he had maintained that interviewing reveals the consistency of responses. In any event, Bewley rebuts the well-known argument of Milton Friedman regarding the irrelevance of a theory's assumptions, maintaining that a deeper understanding is required for successful prediction if conditions change or if one wants to interpret phenomena for policy purposes. Bewley, a respected member of the Econometric Society, concludes that we should supplement existing standard statistical sources with "a kind of main street economics" such as that provided by interviews (p. 352)—shades of what the not generally behaviorally oriented Nobel laureate James Tobin once wrote!

The Schwartz Studies

I have also undertaken several studies based on open-ended interviews. The basic rationale was to explore organizational decision-making. The first study was of 113 medium-size metalworking producers (mainly with the CEOs) in three regions each of Argentina, Mexico, and the United States in 1976–1977 (reported at a UN-sponsored meeting in 1978 and published in 1987). This involved two rounds of open-ended interviews and a third round involving direct observations of ten of the enterprises, the latter lasting from a few hours to as much as four days. Prior to embarking on these interviews, the author read extensively about several of the industries in question and took a one-week course on metal stamping together with officers of metalworking companies at Purdue University. The questions asked of the CEOs varied according to my knowledge of the individual processes—for example, being greater for metal stamping than for ball bearing production—improving as the study progressed and as I visited more plants and became more familiar with the industries under consideration. The period covered was relatively prosperous in all three countries. At the time, I was on leave from the Inter-American Development Bank, and this may have contributed to a favorable reception in Mexico and Argentina.

The second study was undertaken in 1993–1994 with thirty-six Uruguayan manufacturers in a range of industries, at a time when that country was entering into a common market with Argentina, Brazil, and Paraguay. I undertook the initial interviews, and the remainder were handled by an associate, a Uruguayan who had recently completed an MA in economics and had ten years' experience as an accountant. The study was published as an appendix to a book in 1998. I was very familiar with some but not all of the industries. The period was a relatively prosperous one. At the time, I was a visiting professor at the national university in Uruguay.

The third study was with business economists (or, in one case, with an individual functioning in that capacity) in a dozen Fortune 1000 enterprises from the United States (principally manufacturers) in ten essentially monthly sessions during 2002–2003, a relatively prosperous time for the industries covered. The final product was summarized in an article in 2004 and was included with other analyses of the two previous interview-based studies in a chapter of a book published in 2006. The interviews were conducted by telephone and tape-recorded, with notes also taken during the sessions. I was familiar with some though not all of the industries covered. At the time, I was an independent economist.

Another study was based on open-ended interviews over a year (during 2009–2010), with nine primarily small- to medium-size enterprises in Fairfax County, Virginia (a suburb of Washington, DC, of just over one million in population). The period was one of slow national growth following a sharp economic decline. One of those interviewed was familiar with behavioral economics and had taken a course on the subject with a prominent figure in the field in an MBA program. The study was not published. At the time, I was an independent economist. One of the enterprises asked to see articles or books I had published on entrepreneurial decision-making before agreeing to be interviewed. Subsequently, that enterprise allowed me to sit in on a company board meeting.

The results of these studies, involving multiple interviews over extended periods of time, are combined to note behavioral hypotheses about decision-making. With the one exception noted, in the early years of the twenty-first century, none of the respondents (not even the business economists in Fortune 1000 companies) expressed much awareness of behavioral economics, either of the experiments undertaken in laboratories or of field experiments.

4. 2. 1. The Published Studies

4. 2. 1. 1. Findings of the published studies, most of which probably could not have been obtained in laboratory settings (reinforced, in several cases, by findings from the fourth study).

- Even in enterprises that make substantial calculations, rules of thumb are commonly relied upon to complete the determination of their decisions.
- Small and medium enterprises (SMEs) rarely attempt to estimate market demand for prices substantially different from prevailing levels, even when it would seem to be in their financial interest to do so.

- Imperfect perception of some prices and, more importantly, limited recordkeeping lead many SMEs and even a good number of larger enterprises to fail to estimate opportunity costs correctly (though this appears to be less true for financial firms).
- Most SMEs (and many firms of all sizes) do not undertake systematic efforts to improve efficiency. Related to this, businesses tend to be unaware of the degree of slack in their organization until major adversity sets in. More seriously, many business do not provide ongoing efforts for employees to deal with slack; however, many economists in major corporations are relied upon and seek to provide more information about macroeconomic than microeconomic matters. This seems to be more than a matter of the limitations imposed by bounded rationality inasmuch as the enterprises do turn to others in the firm for microeconomic detail and analysis.
- Most SMEs elect not to receive a considerable amount of information that is readily available and that would be in their financial interest to obtain and process. This is true generally and even during periods of moderate upheaval in the economy or in their industry. It did not change much with the recent increase in the ease and the low cost of access to information.
- Profit maximization or high profits objectives do not necessarily lead to attainment of the highest profits feasible. Improved perception of data can lead to higher rates of return even with a reduced profits objective, as can increased coordination that improves the perception of data and eliminates some of the asymmetries in the access to information.
- Enterprise objectives are sometimes multifaceted (which may reflect, in part, taking account of emotional and

mental states), and some of those objectives probably do not allow for increases in profitability. This is in addition to considerations of fairness and reciprocity, which have been addressed in the laboratory.

- Business economists are not active in efforts to alleviate the recognized inconsistencies of accounting conventions with economic principles (e.g., by developing activity-based accounting).

- Although business economists are active in estimating changes in productivity ex post, they do not tend to offer criteria for cost reduction, and they have not made much progress in efforts to develop cost-benefit criteria for innovation projects (and as a rule, for all processes involving more than a few years).

- Most business economists are not asked to participate in corporate evaluations of risk management or in the determination of "hurdle rate" heuristics for the approval of individual projects. Nor do they seem to be disturbed by this; in general, they seem to accept the situation.

- Neither most business economists nor other business executives record the specific heuristics employed or the dimensions of the (often changing) biases associated with those heuristics, even though that information is essential for a good approximation to the complete calculation presumably required for profit maximization. Moreover, the failure to record the way in which some decisions are made increases the uncertainty regarding the degree to which the decision-making reflects largely cognitive or merely more affective heuristics. These concerns hold even for enterprises in which extensive records are kept.

- An understanding of the effectiveness of the way in which businesses respond to obstacles is as important as the identification of the obstacles themselves in determining the best means of designing policies to cope with problems.

These hypotheses should be tested, of course, along with the costs of overcoming the financial penalties involved. The heuristics used in decision-making are considered in the discussion of the fourth study. With respect to the argument of this book (that a behavioral approach should consider what is done by producers and other organizations) and the results of outliers and the averages, note that there are major differences between enterprises in the degree to which the various hypotheses hold, and thus for an industry or an economy's potential rate of growth.

4. 2. 1. 2. Findings of the studies that might be amenable to resolution by laboratory experiments, for which no experiments appear to have been undertaken.

- Differences between stated and realized profits objectives are due in part to a failure to pursue an entirely maximizing process, but also because of the innate difficulty of realizing objectives and particularly because of the failure to take adequate account of uncertainty.
- Most business people do not perceive many marginal differences in financial and economic data. The differences must be large enough to be characterized as "just noticeable differences" to enter into their decision-making—a less significant hypothesis at this point in time because of the widespread use of computers.
- There is a difference in the difficulty in perceiving various categories of data accurately, influenced in part by the nature of the situation, the background of the individual, and the way in which new information is incorporated into the analysis.

- Many business economists refrain from pressing arguments that are valid in economic terms when the CEO or another influential member of the enterprise takes a position contrary to those arguments.

Again, these hypotheses should be subject to tests. In any event, there appear to be major differences between enterprises in the degree to which the hypotheses hold and the importance of the firms in the economy, and thus for the potential growth of the economy—which might be taken into consideration in designing government policy.

4. 3. The Most Recent Study

The most recent study of decision-making processes was based on open-ended interviews with CEOs or other company executives and was conducted by the author in Fairfax County, Virginia, from mid-2011 through early 2012. It was not published but is included, and the results are considered in some detail, first because it reflected an increased amount of experience by the interviewer; second because it was the first study in which one of those interviewed was not only aware of the findings of behavioral economics but also had taken a course from a leader in the field in an MBA program; and third because, similar to the period of the Bewley study referred to, it covered a period of recession, though a much more pronounced one. The period was one of slow recovery from a steep recession that had begun in late 2008. With one exception, the enterprises were SMEs, and with that exception (and perhaps one other), the decisions were made locally (in Fairfax County, Virginia). The county had been a major dot-com boom and bust center in the 1990s and early twenty-first century, but it was not one of the most affected national areas during the recession then in process. The author was more aware of publications in behavioral economics than before and was more experienced in interviewing, but as noted he was not particularly familiar with some of the industries.

The rate of enterprise acceptance of the interview invitations was much lower than in the earlier studies, leading to a sample of firms biased toward those that had been relatively successful in riding out the recession. In all, only nine firms were interviewed. Two were asked if they would permit observation of their daily activities, and one accepted. Each of the interviews lasted an hour. The second round included two taped sessions, but all of the interviews included notes taken during the sessions, which seemed to put several of the respondents more at ease than the sessions that had been recorded. The most revealing session was the observation of a company's board of directors meeting. The enterprises varied from several that had barely survived the economic downturn to two that had thrived and expanded.

The Observation Session

The observation session was held with an enterprise specializing in land development that varied its focus in the face of the housing and macroeconomic collapse, though the firm continued to remain in an aspect of land development and turned to one in which rapid growth was expected and in fact experienced. The discussion at the monthly board meeting revealed two situations in which, though the individuals involved recognized the costs and benefits of the options that needed to be considered, they did not appear to have a rule of thumb for determining the option to be selected. Neither was it obvious how the decisions would have been determined, even with additional time, because the data that would have been required for a fuller calculation were unlikely to become available. The author has encountered similar cases over the years in conversations with entrepreneurs. A lack of enterprise rules of thumb or heuristics for decision-making may be fairly common, especially in fast-moving and successful enterprises. Verification of this would seem to present a serious problem for laboratory experiments.[36]

Although the enterprise interviews revealed a number of results that might have come to light in laboratory experiments, they also provided findings that seem unlikely to have been uncovered with that technique. The most striking finding was that eight of the nine firms did not shift their focus even as the overall economic situation deteriorated, and six of those eight appear to have suffered major financial reverses. In addition, only two of the latter attempted major shifts in marketing or product diversification. Also unlikely to have been revealed in laboratory experiments was that even in the midst of such adversity, most firms did not alter their information search, or they did so only marginally. Note that a few firms reflected clearly outlier and more nearly maximizing behavior. Government policies did take advantage of the diversity of enterprise tendencies but might have done so to an even greater extent.

Enterprise Objectives

The enterprises were not asked directly about their objective (or objectives), but gauging by what was said in a variety of contexts, although almost all sought high levels of profits, only five of the nine seemed to claim that they sought to maximize profits. The manner in which they undertook decision-making suggests revealed objectives that were less than profit maximizing, though in some cases, what was involved may have reflected a perception of maximization in terms of procedural rationality. Yet inconsistency in the way in which decisions were made seem particularly revealing in three cases in which cost reduction was sought only after sharp adversity; there had been little attention to certain costs prior to the downturn. In one enterprise, by far the largest in the group and a firm not based in Fairfax County, a single objective of profit maximization in a traditional sense was particularly questionable because that enterprise had delayed completing a merger for several years due to its judgment that several of the prospective firms were not deemed "culturally compatible." For what it's worth, two of the three firms that most clearly failed to employ optimization techniques (i.e., that reflected a biases approach most nearly coinciding with the decision-making behavior found in laboratory settings for consumers) appear to have been the most profitable. This is somewhat counter to the general thesis presented in this book. The findings may be contrary to Bewley's general conclusion that firms do seek profitability, though his study involved a much larger group of enterprises (and also concentrated on larger enterprises). Perhaps some form of laboratory testing could resolve the matter. In any event, there is a message for government policy measures if the goal is to nudge private sector performance to maximize its contribution to the rate of GDP growth.

The Attitude toward Risk

Only four enterprises emphasized their attitude toward risk; two stated that that they had become decidedly risk averse, and one indicated that it had always been somewhat risk averse and had become more so after the onset of the deep recession. Only one firm claimed to be a risk taker, but my understanding of what all nine did leads me to suspect that two firms fell into this category. Laboratory experiments probably would have uncovered all of these results, at least if the experiments were taken with individuals from business enterprises.

Basic Decision-Making

Only one of those interviewed stated that the firm generally made careful calculations prior to decision-making; the remainder acknowledged that they relied largely on rules of thumb, drawing especially on their past experiences. This would have emerged from laboratory experiments. That includes enterprises that made special mention of the importance of trust and took account of their clients' indication of risk tolerance. One firm emphasized a focus on long term ("not merely myopic") consequences, an awareness of endowment and "disposition effect" tendencies, and maintained that most businesspeople in small enterprises were relatively unsophisticated in the formal techniques of economics and finance. The firm's CEO revealed considerable knowledge of behavioral economics but indicated that in its merger and acquisitions activity, it tended to emphasize cash flow and noted that for its decisions, the firm tried to reduce everything to binary considerations. The latter served as a rule of thumb, though if any biases relevant to the heuristic were recognized, they were not mentioned. It seems unlikely that the complex (and perhaps somewhat contradictory) nature of these factors would have emerged in experiments. This may be in part because different decision-making criteria appear to have been used in different contexts.

Reactions to the Recession and Other Pronounced Economic Changes

All of the firms indicated that they did not anticipate the extent of the economic downturn, though most expected some reversal from the earlier, fairly prolonged prosperity. Most acknowledged that they came to recognize greater risk and uncertainty as the recession continued, becoming more cautious. Fewer than half of them—perhaps no more than two of the nine—changed their form of information search. That failure to react to altered incentives seems unlikely to have been detected in a laboratory setting, and it may be explained by the tradition of a particular, customary way of doing business. Most acknowledged that only in the course of increased adversity had they come to realize that they had not been minimizing costs or taking advantage of all the demand opportunities open to them; other-than-maximizing behavior extended well beyond what might have been expected from inevitable problems of bounded rationality. As a possible example, note that only two of the nine firms increased their purchases of assets in the downturn, when the prices of many of those assets declined sharply, and yet several of the firms that did not do so had available funds or access to bank loans. This behavior, contrary to certain then highly publicized activity of Warren Buffet, may not have been detected in the lab. The more responsive activity of a small minority of the enterprises should serve as a caution against relying on industry averages and is supportive of the general thesis of this book.

Learning

Only three enterprises voiced opinions as to the wisdom of relying on the advice of others familiar with their markets. One was in favor but two were against the idea. One stated that outside opinions were useful only in reinforcing the conclusions of individuals in the firms who, it was contended, were in the best position to judge. Whatever laboratory experiments would have indicated, they probably would have contributed little toward revealing the following lessons that the enterprises claimed that they learned.

Experience led to

- decisions that were made more carefully and more strategically, which means that previously decisions had not been made as carefully and with as much consideration for the long run;
- a greater need to understand others, clients, and competitors, reflecting the importance of trust but also the need for more effective communication;
- a greater recognition of externalities and also systemic (not just specific) risk, with more emphasis than before on loss aversion for all but one of the firms (which did not seem to have a bias toward that phenomenon);
- somewhat greater appreciation that venture capitalists and others who invested only a small portion of their funds in a company tended to not act as much in the interest of the firm as those who invested a large portion of their funds;
- more firms to conclude that similar management styles and other cultural factors should guide merger and acquisition decisions;
- some firms to recognize that downsizing, so emphasized a few years back, may not always lead to increased profitability in the long run;
- a greater need to take account of biases and context in applying rules of thumb and to the significance of emotional factors in sometimes overriding largely cognitive rules of thumb; and
- a greater appreciation of implementation difficulties.

A greater recognition of the need to give more consideration to second-best alternatives. Many but not all of these "learning lessons" were consistent with increased profitability, but most were consistent with the thesis of this presentation that the laboratory findings about consumer behavior did not reflect that of producer outliers.

The Bromiley Study: Extensive Interviews with a Small Number of Enterprises

Bromiley's *Corporate Capital Investment: A Behavioral Approach*[37] is based on interviews with four Fortune 500 companies; one is named, but the others are not, as required by anonymity agreements. The study uses both qualitative and quantitative data dealing with a wide range of topics. The objectives were to understand the corporate planning and implementation process related to investment, to generate a model based on the planning process in one of the firms, and then to use that model to make econometric estimates of investment using data from the other three firms. The study concludes with a framework for the determinants of capital investments.

The analysis includes a number of what Bromiley terms are strategic considerations to the orthodox theory of capital investment. Interviews were conducted with first line supervisors and vice presidents (but not with CEOs).

One chapter provides a detailed examination of a manufacturer of welded and seamless tubing and other steel products. Short-term profit plans were found to influence annual capital expenditures more than long-range plans—an indication of the bottom-up nature of the profit-planning process. A great deal of judgment was involved and several rules of thumb were employed, and though with note of some of the biases, there was no indication as to whether those rules might change over time. Productivity increases were estimated for capital investment, but with rules of thumb that varied. Income forecasts were reviewed at higher enterprise levels, and factors such as financial ratios and market interest rate were taken into account but with apparently inconsistent judgments.

Subsequent chapters deal with the interviews undertaken in the three other firms and the application of the model to them. Bromiley summarizes his findings regarding the investment process, the cash-flow equations, the changes in the hurdle rates for project selection (which were varied only every five years), the (arbitrary) limits on debt, corporate forecasts, asymmetries, constraints on investment, intertemporal differences, interfirm differences, and research strategy. He then compares the relation of his explanation of corporate investment with standard economic theories. He notes that his research raises the question of how to manage the ties between corporate and financial planning systems, and that managers have to deal with complex planning processes that are usually characterized by biased information, multiple interconnecting systems, varying analytical products, and political and managerial concerns. Though Bromiley's conceptual framework captures the details of the planning process well enough to predict investment to a degree that he deems satisfactory, he does not explain the differences or indicate where the differences between the corporate practices he observed and the decisions that traditional economic models would call for reflect rules of thumb that are the best that can be obtained.

The Blinder Project on Price Rigidity

The Blinder project was undertaken together with interviews by three graduate students during the period of 1990–1992. I believe that none of the authors participated in behavioral analyses before or since, and only a few studies even remotely associated with the field were cited. The authors justified the decision to ask business leaders for assessments of what they had done, as well as to have the participants participate in a survey on two grounds. First, it was maintained that traditional economic inquiries had failed to resolve which theories best explained the stickiness of prices. Second, the authors believed that the businessmen would recognize the chain of reasoning that they used. That speculative element differed from the essentially "facts only" approach of the Bewley interviews. The authors defended themselves against the contention that the interview opinions might be unreliable principally by using a number of cross-checks.

Twelve theories of price stickiness were considered, one of which surfaced by the participants in a pretest. The theories were based on the nature of costs, demand, contracts, market data, and market interactions (except, most unfortunately in my opinion, for those involving collusion). Also included was a theory based on the hierarchical structure of large firms. The participants were asked if any important factors were omitted, and none were suggested, though that response may have attributable to the sparse time allowed for comments and the fact that the survey touched on a large number of questions.

Eleven earlier studies of pricing were considered, only one of which was deemed to have had any significant impact on the thinking of economists. Initially, the Blinder study was to have allowed for "free-form" interviews with about twenty companies, with the questions tailored to each company, but it was decided to expand the number to two hundred, and to aim for a random survey sample of GDP to achieve what were considered to be significant conclusions on a national level. Just over 60 percent of the firms contacted agreed to participate, but with the CEO only in the case of the smaller companies. The decision to deal with so many enterprises led to the need for a larger number of interviewers, who, it was maintained, were trained for the task. It was contended that the result was more objective than if a single interviewer had been used. Some questions invited follow-ups, which were provided, but the material was not used in the final evaluation because it was considered statistically unreliable. The questionnaire contained two parts. The first part dealt with the basic enterprise data, and the second examined the twelve theories that might explain price stickiness.

Prices were indeed deemed to be sticky, with 78 percent of GDP repriced quarterly or less frequently, and half of GDP repriced only once a year, though this was during a period of admittedly low inflation. The reasons for this were cited as competitive pressures, a conviction that changing prices would antagonize customers, the cost of changing prices, and the fact that costs had not increased significantly. No evidence was found for the general belief that price increases were more common than decreases, or for the belief that firms reacted more rapidly to cost than to demand factors. Various other conclusions were indicated, and it was noted that the participants' assessments of elasticity and marginal cost were often incorrect.

The twelve theories explaining price stickiness were ranked, with coordination failure receiving the greatest support—although only one-tenth of the firms judged that to be moderately important in explaining the speed of price adjustment. Nonetheless, it was concluded that the theories do a better job of explaining upward than downward price stickiness. The principal observation relating to the findings of behavioral economics was that of fairness in implicit contracts.

The use of interviews did not prove quite as successful as Blinder et al. probably anticipated, but that may have been because of the limited amount of time allowed for the explanations, the failure to attempt to include those explanations in the final analysis (one really wonders about those explanations), and the decision to invite essentially speculative responses rather than ones limited to the more easily ascertainable facts about enterprise decision-making. In any event, the study did establish an argument for the use of in-depth interviews before and after more traditional surveys, and, presumably for laboratory exercises such as those that have become the mainstay of behavioral economics.

Conclusion

These may be the principal results that can turn up in open-ended interview based studies. Some of these results cannot be expected to be revealed in laboratory or field experiments. Both of the latter approaches seem to avoid the verification efforts of such interview-based findings; in the case of laboratory experiments, one prominent researcher maintains that it is possible to deal with any missing concerns simply by running additional experiments, varying the context and laboratory controls. The hypotheses of these interview-based studies need to be substantiated further. In addition, much more attention needs to be given to the way in which organizations make decisions (and the number and type of persons involved in decision-making). Also, guidelines should be established to help ensure that those who undertake interview-based studies are relatively skilled at interviewing and at least somewhat knowledgeable of the activities in which they become involved, or at least of the types of situations they are likely to confront. If they are not entirely objective in demeanor (perhaps too much to expect), they should at least show an inclination to reveal their biases. It should be noted that the responses of the firms in this study differed substantially. Moreover, although the CEO appears to have made all of the basic decisions in some cases, in many enterprises, at least several persons were involved.

CHAPTER 5

The Decision-Making Process of Three Prominent Corporate Leaders and of Organizations Generally

How do organizations actually make decisions? This chapter begins by considering biographies of three prominent American corporate leaders, written by able business journalists but not by economists or others focused on decision-making. It then considers the findings of the interview-based studies referred to in chapter 4, primarily those of this author, and concludes by observing the characteristics of decision-making in organizations generally.

Steve Jobs, Elon Musk, and Jeff Bezos are hardly typical of American businessmen, but in recent decades their enterprises have grown much faster than the economy generally, and they have come to dominate or play a large role in the most of the industries in which their enterprises are found. The same rapid growth also may have held true in the field of artificial intelligence (though the most prominent companies are not owned by the three entrepreneurs considered here). The biographies on which the first part of the chapter draw do not deal explicitly with decision-making, which is certainly a serious limitation from the point of view of this analysis. More strikingly, the decision-making of these major entrepreneurs does not appear to have been studied by behavioral economists to date, even though their enterprises have come to comprise a growing and significant share of GDP. Some of the inclinations of the enterprises of these individuals are not singular among successful entities, as the chapter suggests.

Steve Jobs

There are now quite a few biographies of Steve Jobs. One of these, Walter Isaacson's, which involved a number of interviews with Jobs, deals somewhat more than the others with decision-making and has served as the basis for much that follows.[38] Even so, the extent to which Jobs's decisions prevailed in Apple (and in the other organization in which Jobs was a prominent leader) is not entirely clear.

Steve Jobs was adopted and brought up by a working-class family in California, dropped out of formal registration at an elite college, and then dropped out of college altogether. From the earliest age, he showed interest in the newly evolving field of computers, and at first he collaborated with another individual who was technically more oriented and capable. In periods of difficulty, Jobs declined financial overtures from wealthy industrialists who, although friendly, might have dominated his undertakings. He was a showman, but one who carefully practiced and was usually diplomatic in public.

Jobs described himself as a visionary, and he was much influenced by what might be characterized as intuitive considerations, "not by market research." He stated that he strove to give consumers not what they sought at a given moment of time, but what he believed that they would want in the future when the new products he hoped to create became available. Jobs sought to develop products that would incorporate both technological advances and what he deemed to be artistic merit (in design and beauty), and yet would reflect what he believed was the simplicity that would appeal not just to hobbyists but to consumers who were busy with other matters.

Jobs's idiosyncrasies were accepted due to his extraordinary charisma, his ability to combine technological and design factors, his ability to hire bright, imaginative, and generally outspoken individuals, the attraction of what it was felt that Apple was undertaking, and his apparently remarkable negotiation skills. Although his personal manner was abrupt and sometimes simply inconsiderate (perhaps not always the most effective way of getting things done), and though his views did not always prevail against those of others (whose inclinations also probably did not always coincide with the publicized findings of experimental economics), in most cases, Jobs's decisions appear to have been accepted. Those who worked with him recognized that he was right more often than not (or correct in more important ways), and they seemed to conclude that the large financial and professional rewards was an acceptable price to pay for the control that Jobs sought and exercised, including his inclination to take credit for the company's successes when some of the ideas came from others.

How does what we can say of Jobs's decision-making characteristics coincide with the findings of behavioral economics?

It is difficult to be sure, but Jobs probably valued changes in wealth over the level of wealth particularly because he was not financially well off at the outset of his commercial activities, and in any event, he probably assumed that production of the type of computers he sought would bring him a high level of wealth. Surely he expected losses along the way, and so it is unlikely that he valued losses more than the same dollar amount of gains—the basic characteristic of loss aversion. Jobs was confident, perhaps overconfident, that he could develop the computers he had in mind, and so it is unclear whether he transformed probabilities into prospects, though it would have been hard to estimate the actual probabilities in any event.[39] This must have changed somewhat as the reception of some products in the market was less than he expected; after those experiences, he may have altered his inclination to view and transform market data. He probably had a confirmation bias but did not have a conjunction bias, and he may not have been guilty of the so-called law of small numbers. I would say that he was guilty of overconfidence, but that's not entirely clear despite the mixed acceptance of some of his early products with Apple and Next, given the eventual success of most of the products with which he became involved.

Jobs does not appear to have been guilty of a sunk cost bias. Moreover, he was inclined to take major risks at all times and does not seem to have been concerned by differences in risk premiums. It would not seem that he was sensitive to the accentuation of gains or losses. Data-framing mistakes may have entered in explaining certain losses along the way. Jobs may have seemed to overvalue certainty, but it is unlikely that he viewed it that way.

Jobs did not suffer a status quo bias. He may well have made decisions with data that were only partially relevant, and thus he is likely to have resorted to the use of heuristics, perhaps most notably some variant of availability, but undoubtedly he relied on specific heuristics as well. (What these were is unclear.) Mood swings and emotional factors probably entered into his decision-making. It is unlikely that he put much credence in the efficiency of what he saw in the market, but, at the same time, it does not seem that he paid much attention to inefficiencies in the prices of the inputs he believed that Apple and Next needed and he does not appear to have searched to find the lowest price materials or to have always pushed employees to improve their productivity. Jobs dealt with the future by implicitly assigning very low discount rates, and along with some errors in his judgments about the public's acceptance of the products he viewed as likely to be sought, that explains certain financial setbacks. Fairness, justice, and reciprocity do not appear to have been part of his considerations (in business and in his personal life), and contrary to the findings of the laboratory experiments, he does not appear to have suffered for lack of taking those factors into account.

As important a factor as Jobs was in Apple's decision-making, the final decision-making of the company must have shifted somewhat as the times changed and, more importantly, as the company grew and as Jobs's influence on those who would implement the decisions declined. What is required to ascertain this would be an understanding of shifting organizational decision-making. (Some specialists would disagree that CEOs like Jobs have less influence on employee selection as their companies grow; they would maintain that those CEOs are as able to have their representatives select employees with the same attributes while their enterprises expand as during the first years when the enterprises had only a handful of employees.)

Elon Musk

This account is also based primarily on a biography involving many interviews, including a number with Musk, in this case by the business journalist Ashlee Vance.[40] The biography does not enter into the detail of decisions, but it offers what strike me as a number of relevant considerations.

Musk, a South African by birth, like several other close relatives was an American by choice (in large measure because of his perception that the United States was more open to risk taking than South Africa in the years under consideration). If anything, he is even more egocentric and has a broader vision than was the case for Steve Jobs. He has captured the imagination of Americans (and those in virtually all countries) for his activities with electric automobiles (Tesla), an easier payment system (Pay Pal), solar energy (SolarCity), and particularly his activity in space (SpaceX), which has received many contracts from NASA and envisions travel to and settlement on the planet Mars. All of his commercial activities began as small enterprises that aimed big, and they initially drew sharply adverse reactions, not only from those in the same fields but also from independent outsiders. After a difficult childhood; an early life in Canada, the United States, and South Africa; a pronounced inclination to be bookish and standoffish; and a successful though not especially remarkable college career in Canada and the United States, he emerged as a major but controversial entrepreneur.

Musk has been guided by strong visions of what the future should look like and a desire to do something that will make an impact, perhaps even more than by a desire to make money—though he appears to have assumed that financial success will follow from validation of his other objectives (and whose success he appears to never have doubted). He has sought financial support from private sources and government agencies but has not hesitated to use funds that he has earned, and he has courted bankruptcy on several occasions. He is among the wealthier businessmen at present, a billionaire with prospects for an even brighter position in the future.

Musk is an extraordinary risk taker, apparently highly confident that what he seeks is achievable and that conscientious effort will succeed in bringing it to past. From an initial situation of being reticent to speak in public, success has transformed him into an outspoken and candid individual. Musk seeks out excellence and does not tolerate anything less in those whom he hires or with whom he collaborates. He is often ruthless and unfair in his treatment of employees, but has had little difficulty in hiring those who are exceptionally able or promising (and imaginative) because of his strong and future-oriented visions (almost all of which have been validated or are currently being sought), his personal work ethic, and his willingness and capability for doing that which he hires others to do. Eighty- to ninety-hour workweeks are not uncommon for key employees. People remain with him and admire him, but they do not regard him warmly. Musk appears to have enjoyed good relations with his children and family, but he is divorced and indeed has been divorced several times.

The first major difference in Musk's efforts and the findings of behavioral economics is that, like Jobs, Musk's endeavors do not reflect loss aversion; to the contrary, he seems to have, as his objectives, the proving of certain possibilities, notably those of a desirable and widely used electric car that can overcome the large size and high-cost battery problem and compete with much larger companies, the substantially increased use of less expensive solar energy (abetted by more stylish solar panels), and success with spaceships. Although the amounts of his annual salaries are unclear, he does not seem to be concerned with financial losses along the way (which, indeed, seem to be regarded as an inevitable cost of such endeavors). Whether he modifies probability assessments (and if so, how) is unclear because he seems to be confident of possibilities that others do not visualize, and he has been proven largely correct to date. Musk certainly values changes in wealth more than the level of wealth, but he appears to expect that changes in his level of wealth will follow from achievement of the changes in the goods and societal objectives he regards as feasible.

Musk appears to be guilty of the confirmation bias, and although he would seem to be guilty of overconfidence, his judgments have been validated up to this point, so it is unclear whether he should truly be tagged with overconfidence. He does not appear to be guilty of the law of small numbers or of sunk cost biases, and he does not appear to have a preference for certainty. It is difficult to ascertain any shifts in risk preference or diminishing sensitivity with respect to gains and losses. Similarly, he does not appear to be guilty of the usual framing problems, and he clearly does not have a status quo bias. His instructions to employees have reflected decisions made on the basis of what might appear to be only partially relevant data, but it is difficult to assess some of the instructions because most are not spelled out and probably involve specific heuristics.

Musk's decision-making seems to involve calculation to a considerable degree, but representativeness may be the heuristic on which he most relies. His discounting almost irrationally favors the future in my view, but the discounting may not be traditionally irrational if he is correct about the inevitability of certain possibilities. He seems to have avoided considerations of fairness, justice, and reciprocity, but that does not seem to have impeded his success.

As with Jobs and Apple, Musk's inclinations cannot have explained all of what transpired in the various Musk enterprises; a shifting model of organizational decision-making is called for. Although Musk may have sought to hire individuals who replicated his own decision-making, other styles of making decisions and of dealing with those who implement those decisions were undoubtedly introduced. Finally, note that though the Musk's enterprises have utilized artificial intelligence, they do not appear to have been among the leaders in the field. Moreover, Musk has expressed his opinion that artificial intelligence represents a major threat to civilization as we know it.

Jeff Bezos

Somewhat like Jobs, an entrepreneur whom he admired, Bezos was separated from his biological father while still very young, but he appears to have experienced a comfortable childhood. Many years later, he left the environs of Wall Street to try his hand at developing a website bookstore at a time when books were viewed (correctly) as a declining industry. Amazon has become "the everything store," branching out to merchandise an extraordinary variety of goods and services and evolving as a technology company as much as a retailer.[41] The decision to begin by focusing on books appears to have reflected some heuristic, perhaps some variant of availability, rather than careful calculation. It's possible that Bezos simply saw the opportunity to bring the latest technology to an industry that had been lagging in that respect. Bezos's scope of endeavor has extended even more broadly to include a company that builds spaceships, and perhaps surprisingly, the much more traditional *Washington Post*. The latter may reflect an investment objective or even a prestige objective. Bezos is now into many more activities than either of the other two businessmen considered (most recently leading Amazon to purchase a gourmet grocer and to consider other retail fields), and though success has come more slowly, he has emerged as one of the two wealthiest Americans (now perhaps the wealthiest).

Bezos emphasizes innovation. He works hard and demands the same of those who work for him; he is not interested in hiring or promoting those who want to balance work and home life, though he appears to enjoy a happy home life himself. Although he listens to what his key associates have to say, he does not appear to be tempered by those opinions (not infrequently dealing harshly with those who work for him), and not only does he determine the guiding lines, but he sometimes also exercises final control on what takes place, at least at Amazon, his chief enterprise (although presumably not in entities in which he is only an investor).

Loss aversion does not appear to be a characteristic of Bezos, and his losses have been massive on the way to establishing Amazon as a major player on the American scene. He does not seem to have been particularly concerned by them, although what he earned annually in those periods of company losses is unclear. He appears to value changes in wealth over the overall level of wealth, but at the same time, he seems to have assumed that he will be successful in the long run, and that will lead to a high level of wealth. Note that losses have been incurred not only in ultimately successful undertakings but also in activities that did not pan out as hoped for, at least in the short term. The latter may have served as useful learning exercises.

Bezos does not seem to be guilty of the conjunction bias or the law of small numbers. He is not subject to a status quo bias, and though much of the success of his enterprises has come from insights or calculations on how to operate more efficiently, Bezos appears to bet heavily on innovation. It is unclear whether the way in which he assesses the relevant data involves a transformation of objective possibilities; indeed, the objective probabilities may not be known. He appears to be guilty of overconfidence, but he tries so many more things than most others. He is such a determined fighter that though overconfidence may be involved, it does not appear to have cost him on balance. Bezos appears to be a pronounced and consistent risk taker, and this does not seem to be influenced by certainty or by the possibility of losses or by the composition of his endowment. He does not suffer from a sunk costs bias, but his losses may be explained in part by framing problems. He does not appear to be sensitive to the scope of gains or losses. Bezos appears to have a sense of justice and possibly of reciprocity, but he does not seem to take account of what in this society would be considered fairness. Only occasionally does it appear that he responded differently according to his mood and emotional factors; usually he has taken account of the long-term consequences of decisions.

Even more than in the case of Jobs and Musk, shifting organizational models are called for, and more than a single type, because what takes place in the *Washington Post* undoubtedly has differed from what continues to take place in Amazon (and perhaps in the Bezos space organization).

Artificial Intelligence

There is no single person or corporation to link with the field of artificial intelligence, though Watson and IBM may have come closest in the early period. What seems to be the case is that the exceptionably low discount rate or long-term view has dominated beyond any other explanation. Few other factors can explain the continuing investment in a field in which the return to investment was so low and unpredictable, and few organizations and certainly no individuals would have found such behavior rational in any traditional sense. The only alternative explanation is that a few very influential people have simply insisted on investing in AI whatever the contemporary (and even the expected) return to investment was, which also would have made little sense in any traditional rational sense. That does not mean that a single type of organizational decision-making prevailed in each of the enterprises that had plans in artificial intelligence over the last two generations, however. (Note too that though Musk has voiced negative conclusions with respect to the implications of artificial intelligence for civilization as we know it, he has not hesitated to turn to artificial intelligence to advance certain goals.)

Conclusions of the Interview-Based Studies and Other Interviews

The conclusions on business decision-making that follow are based on the interview-based studies of profit-oriented organizations discussed in chapter 4 and on additional interviews that the author conducted as part of quick studies aimed at identifying prospects for industrial loans, approximately four hundred in number, and half that number of informal conversations, usually fueled by food and drink, that attempted to understand the reasons why businesspeople (generally businessmen) made the decisions that they did. These studies, interviews, and informal conversations differ from the three outlined above in that most of those interviewed were medium-size enterprises, and with the exception of many of those in the Bewley study, more than half were from outside the United States.

The first observation is that the basic decisions usually were made by the CEO (or by a small group), sometimes after receiving advice from a few others in the organization and occasionally from outside consultants. Most of those in the enterprises, even at the department chief level, had no input in the initial decision-making, though subsequent adverse reactions to the decision were taken into account. Some leading officials hesitated to voice differences with the CEO or other key decision makers, even when they were invited to do so; organization economists were notable in this group. Even so, no single model of organizational decision-making would have explained the decision-making that took place.

The decision makers tended to use rules of thumb or heuristics to resolve problems. Only occasionally was there an effort to enter into careful calculation. (Careful calculation might not have been helpful in most cases because of the many uncertainties involved.) The corporations acknowledged their use of general heuristics, and these tended to fall under the heading of representativeness, less frequently anchoring and adjustment, and still less frequently the other general heuristics. They undoubtedly also employed specific heuristics, among the most acknowledged of which was the recent success of a larger corporation that had been confronted by the same problem or opportunity. Although in most cases the enterprises revealed a fairly common response to similar incentives and disincentives, almost invariably there were quite a few outliers. There was rarely a tendency to record the heuristics employed or the biases involved in using those heuristics, even in enterprises that carefully recorded a wide variety of data.

Most decision makers seemed to be interested in producing a

product that was well regarded in the marketplace, but they were at least as interested in achieving a high level of profits. Profit maximization was not an obvious objective, and cost control was random more often than not, so that profit maximization would not have been possible. Bewley, who dealt with somewhat larger enterprises, concluded that there was more concern with cost control and profits (though even some of the quotes in his study suggest that in the past, the corporations had not shown as much concern for costs initially as afterward, when marketplace pressures were greater). Although only a few seemed to have a pronounced status quo bias, past experience (of the organization and of similar organizations) tended to be heavily weighted. Decision makers were generally unable to assess certain relevant pieces of information, and this may have influenced their inclination to modify their evaluation of probabilities, which they did by a variety of means. Moreover, data-framing problems were a problem for many decision makers and they made decisions on partial (though usually relevant) data. A confirmation bias was common, as was use of the "law of small numbers" to reason about the likelihood of certain events, but that was contrary to the experience of the three highly successful entrepreneurs considered earlier. Compared to the results indicated for consumers, however, there was relatively less conjunction bias. There was often a myopic tendency to evaluate prospects over too short a time period (quite unlike the three entrepreneurs and the enterprises active in artificial intelligence described earlier).

Loss aversion was fairly common, and in some cases this was reflected in use of a regret heuristic. There were cases of procrastination, but this was much less common than among consumers, presumably because the cost of procrastination was reasoned to be high.

Most entrepreneurs avoided risk, though they evaluated risk differently for different situations. Mood and emotional considerations entered into decision-making, though to very different degrees for individual decision makers and much less than for consumers.

In sum, the behavioral attributes of leading—and successful—entrepreneurs differs from that of most small and medium enterprises (which register mixed degrees of success), though the latter also differs from the average analysis of consumers. That does not seem to have been much taken into account by behavioral economists, and there is quite a variance among consumers too, as is evident from the available studies of consumer behavior.

CHAPTER 6

The Reality of Producer and Other Organizational Decision-Making— and My Proposals

The thrust of this presentation has been the need for studies in behavioral economics to examine the behavior of organizations— producers, nonprofits, and government entities—and to call for a more open attitude on the part of the behavioral economics community. The underlying assumption of most behavioral economists seems to have been that existing work in the field provides good guidance for all human behavior. The available studies have shown without question that on balance, consumers are loss averse, and they suffer from a number of other biases in their decision-making ability. Such biases differ for individual consumers and need to be estimated (as they have been for loss aversion, one such bias). Each bias may not apply to every individual, and more importantly, they clearly do not apply to all producers.[42] That is particularly relevant if all individuals in an organization do not participate in the decision-making process, and in fact, major decisions are usually the province of a single person or a small group of individuals and do not always take account of the subsequent response of others in the organization or of consumers. There are those who deviate from the average producers—for example, the Steve Jobses, Elon Musks and Jeff Bezoses of this world—and they have been extraordinarily influential in what happens in a society. Moreover, the success of their enterprises, sometimes contrary to at least the short-term interests of community concerns, seems to undermine much that is currently espoused, and it appears to be consistent with the argument of those who are characterized as the most classical of economists: that the only fundamental task of a producer is to maximize profits or to come as close to that objective as possible.

Some deviations from what may be thought of as a financially optimal response to incentives and disincentives may be *intended*, reflecting efforts to take others into account—for example, efforts are under way through MBA-type programs to make the behavior of individuals, corporations, and other organizations more rational in financial terms and even more socially conscious (more in line with broader objectives). Nonetheless, it must be acknowledged that there are limitations in human decision-making and in the decision-making activity of groups, as well as in the ability of humans to show the willpower to stick to the decisions that have been made. More attention should be given to the full range of responses. Although there are areas in which incentives and disincentives draw comparable responses from virtually all involved, there are many other areas in which a variety of responses prevail. And there are areas in which, though most individuals and groups have similar responses, there are some outliers, and the significance of those outliers may be substantial—and not inevitably damaging to the general welfare.

There may well be major financial costs to behavioral responses that reflect biases of note. It may be possible for a society to avoid much of that cost by favoring those who behave "more rationally" (or at least more in line with certain usually government objectives), or by "nudging" all individuals to respond in a particular manner.[43] There are risks of abuse, of course, but it makes sense for the studies of behavior to report the complete findings, not simply to focus on those of the general tendencies. This certainly could be done in analyses of laboratory experiments, and an inclination to do so might provide an incentive to increasing the attention to experiments with those more involved in community undertakings than can be expected from first- and second-year college undergraduates (which remains most common). The latter is likely to involve greater expense than working primarily with college students alone, as is done at present. At the same time, there also might be more of an effort to ask respondents why they chose the options they did—but that would add an interview component to laboratory exercises and, in so doing, increase the demands on those who conduct the studies. That too would add to their cost. An alternative might be to draw on the findings of available interview-based studies, but there are too few to help much. The point is that more can be extracted, even from the existing type of laboratory studies. The same opportunity does not seem to be as available for field or aggregative studies, however.

Now let's focus on organizations alone. Organizations have become increasingly important in our society, not only for what they do directly but also for the options that they make available to individuals as consumers and investors. Here the task is more demanding, so much so that it may not be able to be satisfied altogether—though that is not a justification for not making an attempt.

The only studies that have even begun to uncover the decision-making behavior of organizations have been the handful of interview-based efforts that have been considered in this book. Even so, their concern in attempting to determine why the organizations (private companies, in the case of the available interview-based studies) made the decisions that they did has been primarily to detect aggregate behavior. Some of the behavioral results have differed from the findings of laboratory experiments, as well as the other studies of behavioral economics—the field or natural experiments and the aggregate financial studies. One might have thought that that would have triggered an effort to test the results of the available interview-based studies, but that does not appeared to have happened. The profession that has written about a confirmation bias that afflicts the decisions of individuals seems to have been involved in something similar itself. By the same token, those who have undertaken the interview-based studies may not have paid sufficient attention to the differences in organizational responses—perhaps in part a reflection of the fact that a small number of individuals usually determined the organization's response, and the responses of many of those individuals differed from one another.

The answer, the remedy to behavioral economics not having had as much of an impact as might have been expected, is not to abandon either laboratory experiments or interview-based analyses, but to ensure that both types of analyses report all findings, not simply the overall or average results, and to analyze more carefully the responses to various "nonfinancial" incentives and disincentives.[44] The inclusion of an interview component in laboratory exercises would greatly increase their cost, especially if they were to draw more heavily upon interviewers with real-world experience, some of whom may not have attended college at all, rather than on those now engaged as interviewers. Costs also would be increased, and there would doubtless be a decrease in the number of experiments insofar as those who undertook the studies would have to possess a greater knowledge of the type of organizations they were studying and be more experienced in interviewing techniques. The same would hold for those engaged in interview-based analyses, but there, those requirements might be met more easily, and the new demand would first be that the report of results provide details on the decision-making of the individual or handful of people actually involved. In both cases, costs would be increased, but at the same time, so too would the potential usefulness of the studies.

Beyond that, there would be the extraordinarily difficult task of explaining public and private organizational decision-making. Indeed, it would be necessary to explain different types of decision-making that characterize the organizations at different points in time—not to have an infinite number of explanations, but a certain number to capture the essence of decisions that were made as the contexts, the size, and the relative importance of the organizations also changed. In other words, the task that lies ahead is one of understanding decision-making in public and private organizations of different sizes much better than at present, and to do so over time, which behavioral economists do not seem to have been much concerned with to date. (To begin with, see the insightful writings of Sidney Winter, a follower of Herbert Simon who has continued to be concerned with managerial decision-making.)

In a few cases, it may be possible to rely on authorized biographies, and in other cases, we may have to rely on details provided by disgruntled former employees willing to risk the wrath (and possibly legal suits) of the organizations for which they had worked. This would be a second way of overcoming the surprising and disappointing lack of impact of behavioral economics. Some behavioral economists might even consider listening at length to entrepreneurs (or other organizational officials) before running their experiments. Indeed, a third way of reducing the likelihood that behavioral economics continues to lose its way would be to establish grants for economists (postdoctoral fellowships, perhaps) to spend a year with organizations in order to better understand the ways in which those organizations make their decisions. (Remarkably, of the numerous studies of decision-making, and of the handful dealing with organizational decision-making, none appear to reflect an extended period of listening to and observing the actual decision-making process of organizations.) Such an undertaking also would provide a firmer basis for behavioral game theory. It might even be in the interest of a number of organizations to initiate such an undertaking on their own.

Analyses of these results (or in any event, those that are made public) would be more difficult than the analysis of current behavioral studies, but it is likely to put us in a better position to gauge what will happen to an industry and an economy when incentives change, or at least when certain types of incentives change. In the case of any studies made privately by qualified persons in individual organizations, the results should prove operationally most useful to those organizations.

Conclusion

Behavioral economics has made a major impact in the analysis of human behavior and is enabling a more realistic description of what takes place on the consumer side of the economy. But when one considers the promise of just a few decades back, the field is certainly not accomplishing as much as was expected of it. Moreover, it is not explaining the behavior of organizations sufficiently, and organizations are emerging as important driving forces in the economy. Most serious, behavioral economics doesn't seem to be influencing the direction of the economy as a whole nearly as much as it might.

Behavioral economics is clearly losing its way. Not only does little continue to be done directly on macroeconomics, but the microeconomic research that has been undertaken is ignoring the often important impact of outliers. There's also the fact that relatively few are involved in investigating the decision-making of organizations. Organizations are important in what a society does, and they're becoming more important, even in the options that individual consumers confront. The inclinations of those who determine what organizations do are the ones who matter most, and their biases or the lack thereof, along with the decision-making process in organizations, should be receiving more attention. There does not appear to be a substitute for asking decision makers why they did what they did, and thus for an interview-based approach, though preferably one that devotes much more energy to explaining responses as due to the role of particular individuals or groups.

Organizational decision-making is a complex matter. Behavioral game theory may offer a palliative and may aid in the longer run once more is understood about the way in which organizations actually make decisions. The reaction—or rather, indifference—of the behavioral economics community to interview-based studies and the impressive defense of interviews as a valid empirical approach suggests that any change in recognition of the value of this approach probably awaits pressure from individuals outside the mainstream of the group.

Unless, of course, the behavioral economics community is changing.

Notes

1   Thaler, the 2017 laureate in economics, was the first to implement the seminal work of psychologists Daniel Kahneman and Amos Tversky; more is indicated about their work in chapters 1 and 2. For a lively and revealing account of Kahneman and Tversky by one who came to know them and their families, see Michael Lewis, *The Undoing Project* (New York: W. W. Norton & Company, 2017).

2   Sanjit Dhami, *The Foundations of Behavioral Economic Analysis* (Oxford: Oxford University Press, 2016). This extraordinary contribution has a few omissions, of course, but there is no mention of the important work of Robert H. Frank, especially *Passions within Reason: Human Behavior and the Quest for Status* (New York: Oxford University Press, 1988) and *Choosing the Right Pond: The Strategic Role of Emotions* (New York: W. W. Norton, 1985). There are several other significant omissions. Relevant to the theme of this presentation, there is no note of the important article of Truman Bewley on interviews as a valid empirical tool in economics (cited below, in note 9). Finally, there is no mention of Morris Altman (ed.), *Handbook of Contemporary Behavioral Economics. Foundations and Developments* (Armonk, NY: M. E. Sharpe, 2006), which, despite a few perhaps questionable chapters, provides a stimulating and rather comprehensive introduction to behavioral economics, and one in which two leading contributors to the field question whether the contributions as of the early twenty-first century were truly grappling with much of real world human decision-making. (A confession: I am one of the contributors to the volume.) Also of note is John F. Tomer, *Advanced Introduction to Behavioral Economics* (Cheltenham, UK: Edward Elgar Publishing, 2017), which, though admirable in many respects, suffers from some of the same limitations as the Dhami volume.

3   See the lead article in the May 2015 *Papers and Proceedings* issue of the
    American Economic Review 105, no.5: 1–33, "Behavioral Economics and
    Public Policy: A Pragmatic Perspective," by Raj Chetty. Note that three
    articles in that issue deal with the efforts to teach behavioral economics
    to students by basically incorporating it into the introductory course.
4   See especially Herbert A. Simon, *Models of Bounded Rationality,* 3 vols.
    (Cambridge: MIT Press, 1982, 1997).
5   George A. Akerlof and Robert J. Shiller, *Phishing for Phools: The Economics
    of Manipulation & Deception* (Princeton: Princeton University Press,
    2015).
6   See particularly Daniel Kahneman, *Thinking Fast and Slow* (New York:
    Farrar and Giroux, 2011). They key references are the 1979 article by
    Kahneman and Tversky, "Prospect Theory: An Analysis of Decision
    Under Risk," *Econometrica* 47, no. 2: 263–291, and the 1974 article by
    Amos Tversky and Daniel Kahneman, "Judgment Under Uncertainty:
    Heuristics and Biases," *Science* 185, no.4157 (Sept 26): 1124–1131.
    The breakthrough contributions of Slovic and Lichtenstein dealt with
    preference reversal and first appeared in 1971 and 1973, though later
    versions were not published in economics journals until the 1990s.
    Richard Thaler is the economist who has been most responsible for
    spreading the message of Kahneman and Tversky, undertaking many
    studies on his own or with colleagues, and persuading others to follow
    in his footsteps. See especially Thaler's *Misbehaving. The Making of
    Behavioral Economics* (New York: W. W. Norton & Company, 2015).
7   For an account of the possible differences in the generality of laboratory
    as compared to the field or natural experiments, see Omar Al-Ubaydi and
    John List, "On the Generality of Experimental Results: With a Response
    to Camerer," December 2013, NBER Working Paper W 19666. Though
    one might be inclined to side with Al-Ubaydi and List with respect to
    the generality argument, consider too that individual differences, so
    important to the theme of this presentation, may be clearer in laboratory
    experiments than in many field or natural experiments.
8   See Tomer, *op. cit.* pp. 119–124.
9   I confess to being the author of perhaps the first of these studies. The
    admittedly rudimentary interview-based research "Perception, Judgment
    and Motivation in Manufacturing Enterprises: Findings and Preliminary
    Hypotheses from In-Depth Interviews," *Journal of Economic Behavior
    and Organization* 8, no. 4: 543–565, was published in December 1987,

a decade after the original research was undertaken. In the mid-1990s, the editor of the journal indicated that further research substantiating or refuting the findings was to be considered for publication, but none was ever submitted. The negative comments about this type of research generally were made privately, but see Truman F. Bewley, "Interviews as a Valid Empirical Tool in Economics," *Journal of Socio-Economics* 31, no. 4 (2002): 343–53. This important article also is omitted from the Dahami overview.

10 George A. Akerlof and Robert J. Shiller, *Animal Spirits: How Human Psychology Drives An Economy and Why It Matters for Global Capitalism* (Princeton: Princeton University Press, 2009).

11 Note in particular Thorstein Veblen, *The Theory of the Leisure Class* (New York: Macmillan, 1899), which coined the expression *conspicuous consumption*.

12 Daniel Ellsberg, "Risk, Ambiguity and the Savage Axioms," *Quarterly Journal of Economics* 75, no. 4 (November 1961): 643–661.

13 Kahneman and Tversky, *Prospect Theory*.

14 See especially George Katona, *Psychological Analysis of Economic Behavior* (New York: McGraw Hill, 1951).

15 A collection of Simon's writings can be found in *Models of Bounded Rationality*, cited in note 4.

16 Paul Slovic, "The Construction of Preferences," *American Psychologist* 50, no. 5 (1995): 364–371.

17 *Op. cit*, p. 81, Note, however, that empirical estimates have shown that loss aversion varies widely not only according to context but for individuals. The variance in biases among individuals is one of the points emphasized in this presentation.

18 See George Loewenstein's "Out of Control: Visceral Influences on Behavior," *Organizational Behavior and Human Decision Processes* 65, no. 3 (March 1996): 272–292, and "Emotions in Economic Theory and Economic Behavior," *American Economic Association Papers and Proceedings* 90, no. 2 (May 2000): 426–432. Loewenstein is a professor of psychology, as well as economics, and he has written on a wide number of topics relevant to behavioral economics. Perhaps the psychologist Slovic has been the principal contributor to the affect literature.

19 Gerd Gizerender, *Gut Feelings: The Intelligence of the Unconscious* (2007, New York: Viking). The expanded version to the Gigerenzer approach can be found in Morris Altman (ed.), *Handbook of Behavioural Economics*

and Smart Decision-Making. Rational Decision-Making within the Bounds of Reason (2017, Cheltenhan, UK and Northampton, MA: Edward Elgar), particularly in the initial contributions. Perhaps the best explanation of the approach is in chapter 6, "Heuristics: fast, frugal and smart," by Shabnam Mousavi, Björn Meder, Hansjörg Neth and Reza Kheirandish, although there too the authors might have explained more fully the "transparent and teachable fast and frugal trees" cited on page 109.

20   Max H. Bazerman and Donald A. Moore, *Judgment in Managerial Decision Making*, 8th ed. (Hoboken, NJ: Wiley, 2013).

21   See especially Robert H. Frank, *The Economic Naturalist: In Search of Explanations for Everyday Enigmas* (New York: Basic Books, 2007).

22   For an extended review of the contributions of behavioral economics, see Dahami, *op cit.*, particularly the introductory section (pp. 1–76), the introduction to the nine parts of the book, and the introduction to each of the chapters. The full contents of *The Foundations of Behavioral Economic Analysis* are as follows.

Introduction
Part 1. Behavioral Economics of Risk, Uncertainty and Ambiguity
  1   The Evidence on Human Choice under Risk and Uncertainty
  2   Behavioral Models of Decision Making
  3   Applications of Behavioral Decision Theory
  4   Human Behavior under Ambiguity
Part 2. Other-Regarding Preferences
  5   The Evidence on Human Sociality
  6   Models of Other-Regarding Preferences
  7   Human Morality and Social Identity
  8   Incentives and Other-Regarding Preferences
Part 3. Behavioral Time Discounting
  9   The Evidence on Temporal Human Choice
  10   Behavioral Models of Time Discounting
  11   Applications of Present-Biased Preferences
Part 4. Behavioral Game Theory
  12   The Evidence on Strategic Human Choice
  13   Models of Behavioral Game Theory
Part 5. Behavioral Models of Learning
  14   Evolutionary Game Theory
  15   Models of Learning

23   On the contribution on nonfinancial incentives, see Briggitt C. Madrigan, "Applying Insights from Behavioral Economics to Policy Design," *Annual Review of Economics* (2014): 663–688. See Tomer, *op. cit.*, p. 86 for a list of the ten important types of nudging.

24   See Vincent P. Crawford, "Bounded Rationality versus Optimization-Based Models of Strategic Thinking and Learning in Games, *Journal of Economic Literature* 51, no. 2 (June 2013): 512–527. Crawford indicates that we are still far from the development of full-fledged behavioral models of strategic interaction.

25   Dan Ariely, *Predictably Irrational and the Hidden Forces that Shape Our Decisions,* 2nd ed. (New York: Harper Collins, 2012).

26   Dahami recognizes in his survey that there are differences between individuals in their responses, but he does not consider the possible implications of these differences. Several of the references that he cites recognize that decision-making may come to involve more than a single individual, but they do not pursue the observation.

27   Herbert A. Simon, *Administrative Behavior: A Study of Decision-making Processes in Administrative Organizations* (New York: The Free Press, 1997; first published in 1947). The book was revised three times, the last in 1997, each time with the original text printed separately, and with additional comments reflecting more recent writings of Simon and others. Although Simon took courses in economics for the most part, his doctoral degree was in political science because it is said that he refused to take an accounting course then required for the PhD in economics at the University of Chicago.

28 Simon and a colleague conducted a test that showed that students who were taught a mathematics course with a sequence of problems reflecting increasing difficulty did as well in tests as those who were taught with the theory underlying the problems, contrary to the traditional reasoning that might have been expected. This led him to conclude that there are psychological explanations of learning that extend beyond a mere consideration of results—rather different from what is currently assumed in economics.

29 Josef Maria Rosanas, *Decision Making in an Organizational Context* (New York: Palgrave Macmillan, 2013).

30 Gerald P. Hodgkinson and William H Starbuck (eds.), *The Oxford Handbook of Organizational Decision Making* (New York: Oxford University Press, 2008).

31 Joseph E. Champoux, *Organizational Behavior: Integrating Individuals, Groups and Organizations*, 5th edition (New York: Routledge, 2017).

32 Bewley, "Interviews as a Valid Empirical Tool in Economics," *op.cit.*

33 Bewley, *Why Wages Don't Fall During a Recession* (Cambridge: Harvard University Press, 1999).

34 Schwartz, "Perception, Judgment and Motivation in Manufacturing Enterprises," *op. cit*. Hugh Schwartz, "Appendix B: A Case Study: Entrepreneurial Response to Economic Liberalizations and Integration," in Hugh Schwartz, *Rationality Gone Awry? Decision Making Inconsistent with Economic and Financial Theory* (Westport, CT: Praeger, 1998). Hugh Schwartz, "The Economic Analysis Underlying Corporate Decision Making: What Economists Do When Confronted with Business Realities—And How They Might Improve." *Business Economics* 39, no. 3 (July 2004): 50–69. Hugh Schwartz, "In-Depth Interviews as a Means of Understanding Economic Reasoning," in Morris Altman, *Handbook of Contemporary Behavioral Economics*, *op cit.*, ch. 18: 356–375).

35 Alan S. Blinder, Elie S. D. Canetti, David E. Lebow, and Jeremy R. Rudd, *Asking About Prices: A New Approach to Understanding Price Stickiness* (New York: Russell Sage Foundation, 1998).

36 Returning to the first of the studies referred to above, one enterprise manager allowed me to observe his behavior over the course of four days, initially stating that although he would be happy to talk to me before 8:30 a.m. and after 5:00 p.m., I was to be a silent observer between those hours. Following a difficult decision one day, however, he asked me what I thought of the decision he had made. The year was 1977,

and I was unaware of most of what was to turn up in the professional literature about heuristics. Thinking in terms of a back-of-the-envelope but traditional cost-benefit calculation, I replied that his decision seemed reasonable. Only later did it occur to me that the academic or on-the-job training of many decision makers concerning how to go about problem solving probably remains with them as a kind of default decision rule. This hypothesis seems quite verifiable in the laboratory, though perhaps not the biases that may be involved.

37 Philip Bromiley, *Corporate Capital Investment: A Behavioral Approach* (Cambridge: Cambridge University Press, 1986).

38 Walter Isaacson, *Steve Jobs* (New York: Simon & Schuster, 2011).

39 Overconfidence involves several aspects, but the principal academic analysis for the presence of the phenomenon is that of Malmendier and Tate. In that article, the main measure of CEO overconfidence is the willingness of CEOs to keep their personal wealth undiversified by holding stock market options until very close to the date of expiration. Ulrike Malmendier and Geoffrey Tate, "Behavioral CEOs: The Role of Managerial Overconfidence," *Journal of Economic Perspectives* 29, no. 4 (Fall 2015): 37–60, whose approach would scarcely have sufficed to explain whether Jobs, Musk, and Bezos were subject to the phenomenon.

40 Ashlee Vance, Elon Musk. *Tesla, SpaceX and the Quest for a Fantastic Future*. With New and Updated Material (New York: Harper Collins, 2017).

41 Brad Stone, *The Everything Store: Jeff Bezos and the Age of Amazon* (New York: Back Bay Books, 2014).

42 This is recognized by Laibson and List, but it does not seem to be given all that much importance. See David Laibson and John A. List, "Principles of Behavioral Economics," *Papers and Proceedings, American Economic Review* 105, no. 5 (May 2015): 385–390.

43 The seminal work on nudging is Richard H. Thaler and Cass R. Sunstein's *Nudge: Improving Decisions about Health, Wealth and Happiness* (New Haven, CT: Yale University Press, 2008).

44 Dealing with nonfinancial incentives and disincentives is likely to present difficult problems. The ranking and significance of such factors may vary according to several personal and societal contexts, and it also may vary from one society to another (i.e., from one culture to another).

References

Akerlof, George A., and Robert J. Shiller. 2009. *Animal Spirits: How Human Psychology Drives an Economy and Why It Matters for Global Capitalism.* Princeton, NJ: Princeton University Press.

Akerlof, George A., and Robert J. Shiller. 2015. *Phishing for Phools: The Economics of Manipulation and Deception.* Princeton, NJ: Princeton University Press.

Altman, Morris, ed. 2006. *Handbook of Contemporary Behavioral Economics: Foundations and Developments.* Armonk, NY: M. E. Sharpe.

Altman, Morris, ed. 2017. *Handbook of Behaviourial Economics and Smart Decision-Making: Rational Decision-Making within the Bounds of Reason.* Cheltenham, UK: Edward Elgar.

Al-Ubayaydi, Omar, and John A. List. 2013. "On the Generality of Experimental Results: With a Response to Camerer." (December) NBER Working Paper W19666.

Ariely, Dan. 2012. *Predictably Irrational: The Hidden Forces That Shape Our Decisions.* 2nd ed. New York: Harper Collins.

Bazerman, Max H., and Don A. Moore. 2013. *Judgement in Managerial Decision Making.* 8th ed. Hoboken, NJ: Wiley.

Bewley, Truman F. 1999. *Why Wages Don't Fall During a Recession.* Cambridge: Harvard University Press.

Bewley, Truman F. 2002. "Interviews as a Valid Empirical Tool in Economics." *Journal of Socio-Economics* 31, no. 4: 343–353.

Blinder, Alan, Elie S. D. Canetti, David E. Lebow, and Jeremy R. Rudd. 1998. *Asking About Prices: A New Approach to Understanding Price Stickiness.* New York: Russell Sage Foundation.

Bromiley, Philip. 1986. *Corporate Capital Investment: A Behavioral Approach.* Cambridge: Cambridge University Press.

Champoux, Joseph E. 2017. *Organizational Behavior: Integrating Individuals, Groups and Organizations.* 5th ed. New York: Routledge.

Chetty, Raj. 2015. "Behavioral Economics and Public Policy." *American Economic Review Papers and Proceedings* 105, no. 5 (May): 1–33.

Crawford, Vincent P. 2013. "Bounded Rationality versus Optimization-Based Models of Strategic Thinking and Learning in Games." *Journal of Economic Literature* 51, no. 2 (June): 512–527.

Dhami, Sanjit. 2016. *Foundations of Behavioral Economic Analysis.* Oxford: Oxford University Press.

Ellsberg, Daniel. 1961. "Risk, Ambiguity and the Savage Axioms." *Quarterly Journal of Economics* 75, no. 4 (November): 643–661.

Frank, Robert H. 1985. *Choosing the Right Pond: The Strategic Role of Emotions*. New York: W. W. Norton.

Frank, Robert H. 1988. *Passions within Reason: Human Behavior and the Quest for Status*. New York: Oxford University Press.

Frank, Robert H. 2007. *The Economic Naturalist: In Search of Explanations for Everyday Enigmas*. New York: Basic Books.

Gigerenzer, Gerd. 2007. *Gut Feelings: The Intelligence of the Unconscious*. New York: Viking.

Hodgkinson, Gerald P., and William H. Starbuck, eds. 2008. *The Oxford Handbook of Organizational Decision Making*. New York: Oxford University Press.

Isaacson, Walter. 2011. *Steve Jobs*. New York: Simon and Schuster.

Kahneman, Daniel. 2011. *Thinking Fast and Slow*. New York: Farrar and Giroux.

Kahneman, Daniel and Amos Tversky. 1979. "Prospect Theory: An Analysis of Decision Under Risk." *Econometrica* 47, no. 2 (March): 263–291.

Katona, George. 1951. *Psychological Analysis of Economic Behavior*. New York: McGraw Hill.

Laibson, David, and John A. List. 2015. "Principles of Behavioral Economics." *American Economic Review Papers and Proceedings* 105, no. 5 (May): 385–390.

Lewis, Michael. 2017. *The Undoing Project.* New York: W. W. Norton & Company.

Loewenstein, George. 1996. "Out of control: Visceral Influences on Behavior." *Organizational Behavior and Human Decision Processes* 65, no. 3 (March): 272–292.

Loewenstein, George. 2000. "Emotions in Economic Theory and Economic Behavior." *American Economic Review Papers and Proceedings* 90, no. 2 (May): 426–432.

Madrigan, Briggitt C. 2014. "Applying Insights from Behavioral Economics to Policy Design." *Annual Review of Economics*: 663–688.

Malmendier, Ulrike, and Geoffrey Tate. 2015. "Behavioral CEOs: The Role of Managerial Overconfidence." *Journal of Economic Perspectives* 29, no. 4 (Fall): 37–60.

Rosanas, Josep Maria. 2013. *Decision-Making in an Organizational Context.* New York: Palgrave Macmillan.

Schwartz, Hugh H. 1987. "Perception, Judgment and Motivation in Manufacturing Enterprises: Findings and Preliminary Hypotheses from in-Depth Interviews." *Journal of Economic Behavior and Organization* 8, no. 4 (December): 543–565.

Schwartz, Hugh. 1998. "Appendix B: A Case Study: Entrepreneurial Response to Economic Liberalization and Integration." In Hugh Schwartz, *Rationality Gone Awry? Decision Making*

Inconsistent with Economic and Financial Theory. Westport, CT and London: Praeger, 145–161.

Schwartz, Hugh. 2004. "The Economic Analysis Underlying Corporate Decision Making: What Economists Do When Confronted with Business Realities—And How They Might Improve."*Business Economics* 39, no. 3 (July): 50–69.

Schwartz, Hugh. 2006. "In-Depth Interviews as a Means of Understanding Economic Reasoning." In Morris Altman, ed., *Handbook of Contemporary Behavioral Economics, op. cit.* chapter 18, 356–375.

Simon, Herbert. 1947. *Administrative Behavior: A Study of Decision-making Processes in Administrative Organizations.* With revisions through 1997. New York: The Free Press.

Simon, Herbert. 1982, 1997. *Models of Bounded Rationality.* 3 Vols. Cambridge: MIT Press.

Slovic, Paul. 1995. "The Construction of Preferences." *American Psychologist* 50, no. 5: 364–371.

Stone, Brad. 2014. *The Everything Store: Jeff Bezos and the Age of Amazon.* New York: Back Bay Books, Little Brown and Company.

Thaler, Richard H. 2015. *Misbehaving: The Making of Behavioral Economics.* New York: W. W. Norton & Company.

Thaler, Richard H., and Cass R. Sunstein. 2008. *Nudge: Improving Decisions about Health, Wealth and Happiness.* New Haven, CT: Yale University Press.

Tomer, John F. 2017. *Advanced Introduction to Behavioral Economics.* Cheltenham, UK: Edward Elgar Publishing.

Tversky, Amos, and Daniel Kahneman. 1974. "Judgment under Uncertainty." *Science* 185, no. 4157: 1124–1131.

Vance, Ashlee. 2017. *Elon Musk, Tesla, SpaceX and the Quest for a Fantastic Future.* New York: Harper Collins.

Veblen, Thorstein. 1899. *The Theory of the Leisure Class.* New York: Macmillan.

Index

Names and substantial discussion of topics likely to
be of interest to behavioral economists and others
who are concerned about behavioral matters

About the Author—
and the Book's
Intended Audience

Hugh Schwartz received a PhD in economics from Yale University and taught for a number of years at Yale, Kansas, and Case Western Reserve Universities before joining the Inter-American Development Bank. Subsequently, he was a Fulbright lecturer and visiting professor in Montevideo, Uruguay, and Curitiba, Brazil, and he was a visiting professor in Monterrey, Mexico. He consulted for several private and public organizations. Initially, Schwartz worked as an industrial economist but then shifted to the behavioral field.

Producer and Organizational Decision-Making:
Is Behavioral Economics Losing Its Way?

The book is aimed at behavioral economists and traditional economists, but also at MBAs and the large community of generalists who are concerned about decision-making. The latter have been subjected to limited findings about human behavior and might be inclined to pressure economists to alter studies about decision-making so as to have them take note of the sometimes eventual prominence and even dominance of enterprises that initially were statistical outliers, as well as to reflect what ordinarily takes place when one leaves individual decision-making and turns to the increasingly important organizational behavior. Indeed, it is in the interest of the public to know much more about producer and other organizational behavior, which generally is not the same as that of individual consumers and investors, on which behavioral economics has tended to focus to date.